Isma

Isma Salome Moretz Huffman was age 18 at her wedding in 1913.

Isma

Memoir of a Catawba Valley Family

Kay Huffman Gregory, Editor

Including the full text of Isma Moretz Huffman's

Memories Dedicated to my Grandchildren

GardenDancer Properties, LLC

Granite Falls, North Carolina, USA

Library of Congress Control Number: 2021914877

ISBN: 978-1-7373160-0-8

For more information about this book, contact
Isma.Info21@gmail.com

This expanded, illustrated edition of

Isma Moretz Huffman's memoir

is dedicated to the descendants of those

who once called Middle Little River and

Huffman's Cove their home.

This modern view of Huffman's Cove was taken from Hal and Rachel Huffman's front yard in 2015. Prior to the creation of Lake Hickory in 1928, the Huffman family farmed this fertile bottomland.

Table of Contents

Prologue

Had she been born in the twenty-first century, my grandmother, Isma Moretz Huffman, would have been quite capable of managing a large corporation. Instead, she was born in the late nineteenth century, so she grew up to manage all the challenges of raising, feeding, and clothing a farm family with seven children. In her lifetime, she experienced massive twentieth-century innovations in technology. Electricity, automobiles, airplanes, telephones, refrigeration, and computers – none of these were present in her childhood.

Late in her life, Isma suffered a stroke that partially paralyzed her right side. She lost the use of her right hand, but after physical therapy, she was still able to walk with a limp. Once she recovered from her stroke, her youngest daughter, Millie Kate Huffman Griswold encouraged Isma to tell the story of her life. Isma started writing with her left hand in a spiral bound composition book. Isma Huffman was driven to leave a record of her life for her descendants. When she had completed her work, Millie's oldest daughter, Joyce Griswold Gallagher, painstakingly typed up the often difficult to decipher left-handed writing from her persistent grandmother.

These stories were written with a great deal of determination by a woman who refused to be stilled by the ravages of a stroke. For Christmas 1967, Isma presented her family with the first portion of her autobiography recording her earliest memories to age eighteen, a text she titled "Generation One." Then for Christmas 1972, Isma shared an

1

Oct. 20, 19

Since their has been greater change in the ninetenth century than their had been in eighteen hundred years before I feel I have been privileged to live in the nineteenth century.

I am writing a biography of my life dedicating it to my grandchildren especially to my namesake Amanda Isma Huffman

On a cold frosty morning Jan 14th 1895 the third child a baby girl was born to Lonza Americus Marcy and Mary Louise Iroque Marcy they named the little girl Isma Salome Marcy

Did you ever sit down and try to think of the first thing you can remember in your life be honest with your self and say it sometime it is not as easy as you might think.

the earliest thing I can remember was setting on the floor and holding my baby brother his name was edward I was two and a half years older than he, and he died before he was a year old so guess I was about three years old

Here is Isma Huffman's left-handed handwriting after the stroke paralyzed her right hand. She started at the back of a composition book and worked her way to the front. When she wrote "Generation Two," she continued writing in this same notebook.

expanded autobiography that recorded her married life with Arthur Huffman while living on Huffman's Cove with a significant detour to Wyoming! This portion of the book is titled "Generation Two."

In recent years, old family pictures have captivated my imagination. I realized that Grandma Isma's book would be even more riveting with the addition of photographs to illustrate her words. As I entered page after page of Grandma Isma's story into my computer, I was careful to leave her word choice and sentence structure in its original format. I want present day readers to hear Grandma's distinctive voice. Spelling and punctuation errors have been corrected. Any clarifications I made in the text are enclosed in brackets.

As an epilogue to Isma's book, several of Arthur and Isma Huffman's children and grandchildren have shared some of their memories to pass down to future generations. This section of the book is titled "Generation Three." These descendants each speak from their personal time roaming the pastures, hills, creeks, and lakeside of Huffman's Cove under Arthur and Isma's watchful eyes.

The blending of the Huffman and Moretz families described in this book happened in the foothills of the Appalachian Mountains in Western North Carolina. The marriage of Isma Salome Moretz and Arthur William Huffman over a century ago on February 9, 1913, established the family framework. Both family lines originated in the Palatinate Region between Germany and France. Both Huffman and Moretz ancestors had migrated to the United States to escape religious persecution and to pursue a more prosperous life.

Isma was eighteen, and Arthur was twenty-five and just returned from his first set of Wyoming adventures when they were married in 1913.

The extended Huffman family and the extended Moretz family were a significant force in the social and financial fabric of Western North Carolina. They were resourceful, hard-working people. They cared for the land that sustained them, and the flowing waters of the Catawba River basin is integral to their history.

The Moretz ancestors settled all along various tributaries of the Catawba River. They built water-powered mills for sawing lumber and grinding grain. Isma Moretz grew up on one of those tributaries, the Middle Little River. Just downstream, her Uncle Tom Moretz ran the local water-powered sawmill. The Western North Carolina patriarch of the Moretz clan, John Moretz, Sr., established several mills and various business enterprises in the Boone, North Carolina, area. One of his grandsons, Alonzo Americus Moretz, was Isma's father and one of my great-grandfathers.

Likewise, the Huffman family ancestors played their role in local society and business. Isma's father-in-law and another of my great-grandfathers was Daniel Monroe Huffman. Daniel was a well-respected, self-taught veterinarian whose skills helped local farmers maintain their livestock. The five green hills at Huffman's Cove on Lake Hickory today once surrounded rich bottomland located about half a mile from the main channel of the Catawba River. In 1928, that bottomland became Huffman's Cove, and the hills became lake front property when Duke Power Company built the Oxford Dam and the water impounded to form Lake Hickory. Arthur Huffman ran a fishing pier on Huffman's Cove for several years in the 1940's and 50's.

With the relentless passage of time, some physical evidence for this story remains as nature leaves her impartial historical record. One of the giant oak trees still stands above Huffman's Cove sinking its roots deep in what was once Arthur and Isma's front yard. The waters of Huffman's Cove still sparkle in the sunlight.

Family lunch under the oaks, circa 1958.

After one hundred and twenty years, parts of the stacked rock retaining wall built by Alonzo Moretz border the edge of Moretz Lake in 2021.

Over in Alexander County, some of the stacked rock walls built by Alonzo Moretz in the 1890's still stand along the edge of Moretz Lake. A walk down the steep north-facing hill reveals the remains of the springhouse location that was upgraded with a trolley system by Mary's father Elijah Wilson Teague and Alonzo's father, Zechariah Taylor Moretz.

Today, the waters of Middle Little River still flow into Moretz Lake behind the barrier of Moretz Dam. My father, Hal Huffman, owned farmland just across the lake from where his mother Isma and her family lived in the 1890's and early 1900's. When I visit that same land

The Middle Little River provides a lovely spot for a family outing.

today, I enjoy staring into those waters. Sometimes, I fancy that I hear the young voices of Mary and Alonzo's children playing on the river sandbar. It is a comfort to know that when my grandchildren play in Middle Little River, they make the eighth generation to stare into those waters tracing from John Moretz, Sr., the second generation Moretz ancestor in America.

Isma Moretz Huffman completed through sixth grade at the local one-room schoolhouse, the highest level available in the area at that time. A lifelong avid reader, she was a highly educated and capable person. She reputedly read all the volumes of the *World Book Encyclopedia* that she and her husband purchased with installment payments. She is also known to have read the dictionary too! Her stories range from detailed descriptions on how to dry fruit and how to make soap to tender family stories of women who spent both daylight and evening hours cooking, washing, and sewing for their families. Family love and affection shine throughout these humble tales. This book is an authentic, unvarnished history of daily life in the Catawba River Valley from 1895 to 1974.

Kay Huffman Gregory, Editor
A Granddaughter of Isma Moretz Huffman
May 2021

Memories Dedicated

To My

Grandchildren

Since there has been a greater change in the twentieth century than there had been in eighteen hundred years, I feel I have been privileged to live in the twentieth century.

I am writing an autobiography of my life, beginning with my first memories through my seventy-sixth year, dedicating it to my grandchildren, especially to my namesake Amanda Isma Huffman.

Isma Moretz Huffman

Hickory, North Carolina

1972

Isma Huffman started writing her manuscript in October 1967.

Middle Little River, 2020

Generation One

On a cold, frosty morning, January 14, 1895, the third child, a baby girl, was born to Alonzo Americus Moretz and Mary Louise Teague Moretz. They named their little girl Isma Salome Moretz.

Did you ever sit down and try to think of the first thing you can remember in your life? Be honest with yourself and try it sometime. It is not as easy as you might think.

The earliest thing I can remember was sitting on the floor and holding my baby brother. His name was Edward. I was two and one-half years older than he, and he died before he was a year old, so I guess I was about three years old.

Another thing I can remember was something my great-grandmother did for me. She picked a pan of raspberries and sat me down on the floor of the porch and put them on my lap and would not let Artie and Arthur, my sister and brother, take them away from me. I can remember how she looked. She always wore a cape. I have one of her Sunday capes which is black embossed wool worsted with lace around it.

Isma gave her great-grandmother's Sunday cape to her namesake, Amanda Isma Huffman Hall. The breast pin belonged to Isma's mother, Mary Teague Moretz.

We lived on a little rocky farm of fifty-nine acres on Middle Little River. My father was a thrifty man. He not only farmed but was a carpenter and a brick mason. They did not have much fertilizer in the old days, and people cleared new ground to get better crops.

I remember one of the highlights of my childhood was when we had a log rolling and a quilting. The neighbor men came and rolled logs together in the new cleared ground and burned them. Their wives came along and quilted a quilt. Mother and some of the other women brought in the big iron wash pot and set it before the big kitchen fireplace and filled it about two-thirds full of chicken and spare ribs and gravy. Then about a half-dozen women went to the kitchen to stretch dumplings. In a little while the men came in tired, sooty, and hungry, and all had a good old-fashioned chicken and pork dumpling supper. They had a lot of good fellowship, and then all went home tired, but happy.

This is my first experience working in the field. It was wheat harvest, and in those days, you cut wheat with a scythe and cradle. Daddy was cutting; Mother was binding it in bundles; Arthur was carrying the bundles, a dozen to a pile. Then they would set them up. Artie was baby sitting with Carl. They told me I could be Ruth gleaning in the fields of Boaz. I didn't have the slightest idea what that meant, but I sure did pick up a large pile of wheat heads. I didn't want to put them in the shock with the others, so they said I could take them home and give them to the old roosters we had penned up to fatten. Let me tell you what kind of chickens we had. They are called Barred Rocks now, but back then people called them Dommerneckers [Dominickers]. They were lighter in color and larger. A fat rooster would weigh ten or twelve pounds. When you killed one, you thought you had a turkey. You can see why I picked up so many wheat heads.

While I have been telling you about harvest, let me tell you about wheat threshing. When the wheat bundles got good and dry in the shock, they would haul them in the wagon to the barn and stack them in ricks in the barn loft. Then the threshers would come. They pulled the machine that threshed the wheat with a team of mules from one farm to another. They used four teams of mules to go round and round to turn the machine that turned the gin that threshed the wheat. About 1905, they got a steam engine to do the work instead of mules. Neighbors always helped each other at threshing time. The women helped each other too.

There were always ten or twelve hungry men to feed – one, two and sometimes three meals. You could not prepare food ahead of time like we can today. There were no refrigerators, no ice, just what you could keep in your springhouse, and you could not keep things too long.

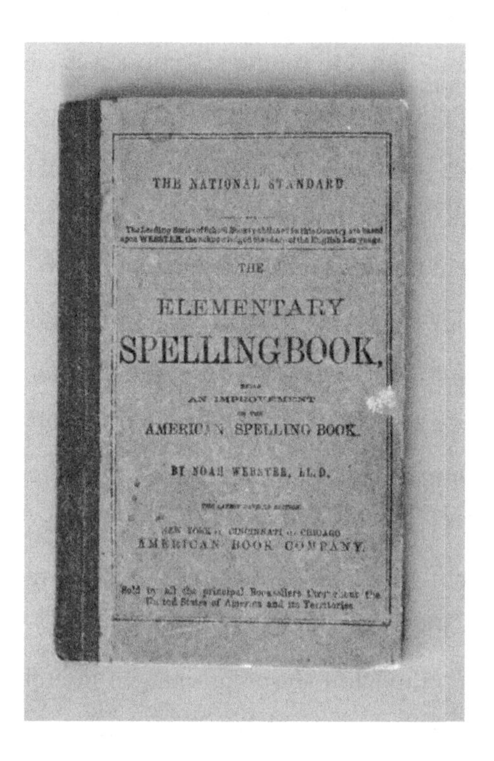

Isma valued education. She kept her speller from the one-room school.

In the year 1900, I started to school. We just went four months out of the year -- November, December, January and February. The school house was just one little room with a big fireplace about six feet wide at one end of the room and a door at the other end with a shelf outside the door with a large bucket of water with a dipper in it for the children to drink from. There were just two windows on each side of the room for light, with an aisle up the middle with five seats on each side. The little ones sat on the front seats and the oldest ones on the back seats and the other ages in between. More about school later.

The winter of 1900 and 1901, my father was taken sick. He wasn't bedfast till March, but he was not able to work. In those days, the doctor came to your home, so my Grandfather Moretz got Dr. Henry Abernathy to come to see my father. Doctors had no way to travel but by horseback, so he ate dinner with us. My mother had cooked shuck beans or dried green beans. Some people called them leather britches. She said she didn't know whether to put them on the table or not, so she put them on the far side of the table. That was the first thing that Dr. Abernathy reached for. She never saw anyone eat so many leather britches.

School was out the first of March, and my daddy thought he wanted to go down to the river and fish one sunny day, but he was so weak he could hardly get up the hill to the house. I was just six years old, but I can remember the big beads of perspiration standing out on his forehead. I guess with four children in the house, ages one through ten, we were pretty noisy, and I guess I was at the noisiest age. My father was getting worse all the time, so my Grandfather Moretz took me home with him to stay a few weeks. My grandfather was so good to me I didn't get homesick. Grandfather lived in Hickory about one and one-half miles southwest of the Piedmont Wagon Company. He tended a small farm, and my Uncles Titus and John worked in town. Grandmother had a sister who lived close by. Her little nephew lived with her, so she let him come play with me most every day. That is why I didn't get homesick. On the

Zechariah Taylor Moretz (1846-1911), second generation from John Moretz, Sr., and Harriet C. Bowman Moretz were Isma's paternal grandparents.

morning of April 10th, my grandfather said we would go home and see how my father was and take the mules home so my uncles could plant our corn. We had got about halfway home when we met my Uncle John coming to tell us my father had died that morning.

I arrived home with mixed emotions. I had not seen my family in two weeks, which is a long time for a six-year-old who had never been away from home before. When my mother came out and hugged and kissed me, I was sad about Father, but so glad to see my family. I don't know whether I laughed or cried. I do know I got Carl, my baby brother, on my back and ran to the barn and back till I fell down and skinned my knees. I can't remember too much about my father at home before the funeral. I remember seeing the wagon with the casket on it going in front of us and when they opened the casket at the church. I remember Rev. Alonzo Downs preached the funeral. Father was buried at Friendship Lutheran Church in Alexander County.

The next few weeks were the saddest, most lonesome weeks of my life, and I know it must have been terrible for Mother, but she could not nurse her grief. There were four children she had to feed and clothe, and it was the time of year to plant a crop. Our grandfathers planted the crop and would use our mules to work for pay. It would always be night when they would get them home. We would always sit on the porch waiting and listening for the wagon, Mother sitting on a little low rocker with Carl on her lap. Arthur, Artie, and myself huddled on the floor at her feet hearing the whippoorwills and owls hollering in the woods nearby. You know it was lonesome. I am almost seventy-three, and it is indelibly on my mind yet.

My father was just thirty-three when he died. He was born April 23, 1868, and he was married April 30, 1890. He died April 10, 1901. He and Mother had been married ten years. They had bought fifty-nine acres of land and paid for it. They built a house, granary and barn, and a chicken house. They had also fenced and crossed fenced the field on the backside of the farm. I forgot to tell these fences were built with rails that he had to split. He set out an orchard of apple, peach and pear trees. We had fruit from June through October.

I think the neatest things he made were the grape vineyard and garden fence. There were six rows of grapevines with twelve to the row. Each vine had a post with crosspieces on it. It sure looked pretty, and we

Alonzo Americus Moretz (1868-1901), third generation from John Moretz, Sr., accomplished a great deal in his brief life.

got a lot of pretty grapes. The garden was the thing I enjoyed most. You didn't have wire in those days, so Daddy built a paling fence. It was one hundred-fifty by one hundred-fifty. It was just at the backside of the kitchen and always had things growing in it. On the far side from the kitchen, we had raspberries planted on the outside of the palings, and a strawberry bed about ten feet wide on the inside. Along the backside,

Mama had her herbs growing: mint, tansy, sage, ground ivy, catnip, coriander, sweet basil and thyme. Just mostly what the chickens would eat was planted in the [kitchen] garden. We had what the old timers called truck patches for the other vegetables such as Irish and sweet potatoes, corn, cane, peas and beans for dried beans, and peanuts.

There were two other things my father built that were a lot of help to us in the years ahead, which were a dry kiln and a springhouse. I will tell you about the dry kiln first. I will tell you what it was for. I don't believe either of you has seen one. It was to dry apples and peaches in the summer when it was cloudy and rainy. Everyone who had an orchard had a dry kiln. It was built with rocks all but the roof. It was about ten feet long and six feet wide and five feet high, up to where the roof slanted to the backside. There was a furnace the length of the kiln with a flue at the back end and open at the front to fire the furnace. You could burn six to eight foot pieces of wood in our kiln. There was a door the length of the kiln on the front side that was hinged at the bottom so you could turn it down out of the way when you filled the kiln. There were four iron rods that ran the length of the kiln to sit the dry boxes on to dry the fruit. There was always a market for dried fruit, and we had a large orchard. We always hauled in a large pile of wood during the winter to have it ready when the fruit was ripe.

Now I will tell you about the springhouse about one hundred-fifty yards from the house. Under the north side of the hill was the spring. It was at the very bottom of the hill. There was a big laurel tree on either side of the spring. It had leaves and blooms like a magnolia, only they were pink. About six feet from the spring was the springhouse. It was eight by six feet with a cement floor and a box eight inches deep on the backside for the water from the spring to run through so we could set our milk in it to keep cool and sweet. The first four feet of the wall was built of rock, and then the rest of the wall was built of slats two inches wide and one inch apart. A roof slanted to the back.

I think that about takes care of the things my father built, but I want to mention a few material things he left his family, which were a good team of mules, wagon and farm tools, two cows, fifteen sheep, a brood sow, and a large flock of chickens.

I think that next to my family, the church is the closest to my heart. I think the sweetest memories I have of my father is his leading singing in the Old Fellowship Church. The church that is there now is the third in my lifetime. There is one service I especially remember. It was a communion service. They had fixed up a table and set it up down the aisle from the pulpit to the door. Then they put benches on each side, and the people sat around the table, and they passed the bread and wine around. I remember Reverend Cottrell put a chair at the head of the table and said that was for Jesus. He was our unseen guest. I felt too awe-stricken. I would not have moved and made any noise for the world. I guess I was about six years old.

They always had a revival the second week in August. They would have all-day service and would spread their dinner out together in a couple of wagon beds. One member, Bob Barnhill, always brought watermelons and cantaloupes for dessert. We just had services once a month on Saturday evening and eleven o'clock on Sunday.

Mary Louise Teague Moretz, circa 1890. After her husband's death in 1901, she raised her four children alone on a small Alexander County farm that bordered the Middle Little River.

About 1903, we had our first Sunday School just in the summer months. Most everyone had to walk or ride in an open wagon. It lasted from May through October.

My Grandpa and Grandma Teague had come to spend the night, and we were going to butcher our hog the next day. We got through, and we had sat down to eat dinner when Grandpa Moretz came by to get the mules. The Grandpas got to talking, and they thought that the spring path was too steep for us to carry water up, so they decided to make us a trolley. Grandpa Moretz was a carpenter. He was to make the large wheel to wind the rope on the trolley to carry the bucket and the box for the bucket to dip in. Grandpa Teague was to furnish the wire for the trolley to run on [and] the rope to pull the bucket as well as put up the posts and clean out a new spring. After they had decided what they wanted to do, they decided where the spring box would be put and where the posts would be put. The next week Grandpa Teague and Uncle Fate, that was Mother's brother, came and cut the posts and set them and cleaned out a new spring and had everything ready when Grandpa Moretz came with the trolley and bucket and wheel. We sure did enjoy using it. Mother was never without water.

The fall of 1902, I started my second year of school. My horizons began to widen. I knew more people and began to pick out friends. I will give you the names of the families that lived on the southeast side of the school that walked the same road we did till each took the path from the highway to their home. There were five families that lived on this side of the school. My Uncle Webster Moretz lived the farthest away. He lived across the river from us. There were four children in school from that

The remains of the old spring site still mark a boldly flowing water source. The rocks are mainly collapsed after the passage of more than a century.

home. Their names were Lee, Stella, Mamie, and Pearl. The next family was Bob Barnhill. They had two boys, Manuel and Fred. Next was Waitsel Austin. They had five children, four old enough to go to school. They were Press, Partee, Bertha, Mertie and Naomi. Last was the Wess Miller family. There were eight children, just six old enough to go to school. Their names were Elmore, Rob, Letha, Lilie, Mattie, Dorothy, Ray and Perry. Mr. Miller was a tall, skinny, friendly man who ran a blacksmith shop. His shop was close beside the road, and he could fix anything that needed fixing on the farm from shoeing your horse and fixing your wagon wheel to sharpening your ax. We children loved to see him shoe horses. He would trim the hoof and run the bellows, getting the shoe hot so he could fit a cork on the back of the shoe so the horse's foot would not slip when he was pulling.

There were no school children in this family, but she was a neighbor who everybody would have missed if she would not have been there. Her name was Liza Bowman. We always called her Aunt Liza. She was a widow. Her husband was killed in the War Between the States. When any of us children got sick, Mother would always send for Aunt Liza, and she would always come bringing herbs and home remedies with her. Sometimes she would stay all night if we were very sick.

I shall always remember the night I spent with her. When Mother would go to spend the night with her parents, the Grandpa Teague's, Artie or I would stay home and do the chores and spend the night with a neighbor, so I said I wanted to stay with Aunt Liza. I had always admired her beds. They were tall, four poster beds – at least four feet up to the rail. They were cord beds. She always had them made up so pretty with hand-made wool coverlets on top with hand-tied fringe on underneath sheets. The fringe would be showing about six inches below the coverlet. When I got in the bed that night, I was like Granny in the Hillbillie's. [A reference to a television sitcom, *The Beverly Hillbillies*, that aired 1962 – 1971.] I thought I had gone to heaven. There was a feather bed on top of the mattress, then a nice soft comforter on that, then your sheets and a little soft quilt. When I laid down on that, I felt like I was floating away in the clouds. Needless to say, I slept like a log. When I awoke, Aunt Liza was up and had built a fire in the fireplace and was fixing breakfast. Like everybody in those days, she had a wide hearth in her kitchen and was cooking by the fireplace. She had a stove, but in cold weather, she cooked by the fireplace. She had a little skillet with legs about three inches long. She shoveled out live coals on the hearth and set the skillet on the coals and put a couple slices of ham in the skillet. Boy did that smell good and taste better with a piece of sour dough bread baked in the skillet by the fireplace. Before she sat down to eat, she filled the skillet with sweet potatoes and put fresh coals on the lid till we finished breakfast and washed the dishes, and I was ready to go home. She wrapped up a potato for each pocket. She said they would keep my hands warm and would taste good later in the day. Now you can see why a ten-year-old girl loved to spend the night with a seventy-year-old woman.

Now I will get back to telling about my home life. The spring my father died, my mother had to work so hard with the garden to plant and field crops to plant. After the crops were all planted, about the middle of May, she had to shear the sheep. I would always sit at the door of the stable and watch her clip the wool off the sheep. They looked so ugly when that thick fleece of wool was first taken off. We would put them in a good warm stable till they got used to their fleece being taken off. We would put the mother sheep up when they had a little lamb. They were the sweetest, [most] innocent looking animals I know. The mother would stomp her foot at us when we came near when the lambs were small, but in a few weeks, we could hold them in our arms.

Mother didn't like shearing sheep, so she sold them all but six, just enough to get wool for our stockings. She sold one of the mules and the two-horse wagon and bought a one-horse wagon. Arthur could handle the one mule, so now we could go to church and to our Grandpas and our kinfolks. Mother and Arthur would go to Hickory about twice a week that summer with a load of peaches. Our young orchard had just begun to bear. We would gather the peaches the evening before and have them loaded in the wagon so Mother and Arthur could leave early, sometimes before sun-up, so they could sell their peaches and get home before dark. Artie, Carl, and myself stayed home. Mother always had a job for us. If we got done before night, we could go to Uncle Tom's and play with our cousins. Sometimes we had to hoe the peanuts, or a patch of corn or peas. On this particular day, it was to halve peaches and put them out to dry. In case you don't know what halving peaches is, I will inform you. Back in those days, most every farm had a few trees of these peaches. They were little open stones about one inch in diameter. You just cut them in half to take out the seed and put them out on the dry boxes to dry with seed side up. It took almost as long to lay them out to dry as it did to halve them. Mother told Arthur to go and shake the peach trees so we would have some work to do while they were gone. We had six trees of that particular kind, and I think he tried to shake them all off. We were still halving peaches when they came home that evening, but we were happy.

Mother had bought material to make us dresses, and she said if we would be smart and help take care of the fruit, she would take us along to Hickory when the circus came to town that fall, and we would have a group picture made of the family, and we would spend the night at our Grandpa Moretz's. That was a treat to look forward to when you remember that we had not been there since our father's death, as we had no way to travel till we bought the one-horse wagon. Mother kept her

After Alonzo's death in April 1901 and after a summer of hard work, Mary rewarded her children with a trip to the circus complete with new clothes and a family portrait. Left to right: Isma Salome, 6; Arthur Taylor, 10; Mary Louise Teague Moretz; Carl William Moretz, 1; and Artie Naomi, 8.

promise. Every chance she could get away from the farm work and taking care of the fruits from the orchard, she was sewing, making the dresses for us to have our pictures made in. I think of all the dresses I have had in my seventy-three years, I liked that one best. If you don't believe it was pretty, come and I will show you the picture. Let me tell you how they were made. The material was navy blue wool worsted. It had a square plush velvet yoke with satin ribbon gathered in the middle all the way around the yoke. It had a gored skirt set to the waist with a band.

Well, at last the big day had come. Ads on all the country stores and along the public roads said the circus was coming to Hickory on September 30th. Mother got all our clothes ready, and we got a neighbor to take care of our cows and chickens and hogs. We were ready to go at five o'clock. We had to cross the river in a ferryboat. It took about ten minutes to go across, so you see if there were a half dozen ahead of you, it meant waiting a good while. We got there about sun-up. No one was ahead of us. We were in town about ten o'clock. Mother bought Artie and me button shoes and hair ribbons to have our pictures made in. We went into MacEntash's Studio, primped up, and we had our pictures taken. We got through in time to see the parade. It was my first time to see an elephant, camel, monkey, bear, and all the pretty horses, clowns – it sure was an exciting day for me. We went to the hitching lot. That was the place you tied up your horse and left your wagon while you were shopping. We didn't have time to eat our dinner before the parade, so we were about starved. You could not buy hamburgers and hot dogs. In fact, you could not buy anything to eat without going to a restaurant. We had brought a basket of dinner with us, so that ham biscuit, boiled eggs, and peach pie tasted mighty good at two o'clock in the afternoon.

After we finished dinner, we got settled in the wagon and started for Grandpa's. He lived about three miles from downtown Hickory, south of Piedmont Wagon Company.

We had more excitement when we got there. I saw my Aunt Nora and Aunt Jina for the first time. I knew about them, but I had never seen them. Grandpa Moretz had moved to Chicago the year Mother and Father were married. Grandpa and part of the family moved back to Hickory in 1900. Three of the aunts stayed in Chicago – Aunt Jina, Aunt Nora, and Aunt Salome. Aunt Salome married Ed Welble and died out there. I never saw her. She is the aunt that named me. Aunt Nora and Aunt Jina were home. I shall never forget how pretty their living room looked to me. We never had much, only the bare necessities at home which were beds, tables and chairs, and one little low rocker. They had a lounge and three or four pretty rockers and a rug on the floor. Artie, Carl and I sat on those rockers and sang "mine is the prettiest, mine is the prettiest." Mother had to quiet us down, and we soon went to sleep. I don't remember supper. Maybe we went to sleep without supper. We surely had enough excitement for one day. I can remember breakfast, not so much what we ate, as what we ate it out of. I had never seen any real china and silver. Aunt Jina and Aunt Nora each had a set. Aunt Nora's was blue willow, but Aunt Jina's was the daintiest and thinnest, prettiest I have ever seen. It was what we ate out of that morning. When my fork or knife would touch my plate, it would ring till I thought I had broken it. That morning about ten o'clock we started home. Grandma filled our basket with food for our dinner. She could make the best baking powder biscuits I ever ate. She had a lot of them in the basket, and that was the first bologna I ever ate. With those biscuits, it sure tasted good to me.

We got home about four o'clock. The next day we went to picking peas. We had white peas we always raised for eating and three or four bushels extra to sell. We could get twice as much for them as the colored [peas]. We had to pick them as soon as they got ripe. If it rained a couple days, they were not worth picking, so Mother taught us when we were young that it didn't take as much time to do a thing when it was ready than to wait till later.

It was molasses-making time. We had the nicest crop of cane we had ever had. We had to haul our cane to a neighbor, Wess Miller. He is the man with the blacksmith shop. He had a cane mill and boiler. You could use his equipment and let him have molasses for pay. We had pressed out a boiler of juice and got the boiler started. You had to furnish your own wood, and Arthur and I left Mother with the boiler and went to the sawmill to get a load of slabs. It was at the noon hour, and Uncle Tom had gone to dinner. Just as quick as he went in the house, Arthur went to looking things over. The mill was run by waterpower. He didn't dare turn on the water, but he got up on the belt that ran the shingle saw. It was a little saw about one foot in diameter that ripped up the shingles when they were sawed in slabs. He got the saw to running from tramping the belt. He hollered to me and said, "Look at it go." I ran over there and stuck my left hand right down in it between the guard and the saw. He jumped off the belt and turned the saw backward and got my hand out. It had ripped my little finger on top till you could see the bone in five places where the teeth of the saw had cut across the top of my hand. Arthur was afraid to tell Uncle Tom, so we went to the spring and tried to wash the blood off. Uncle Tom came back and said, "Boy, I have a notion to give you a good thrashing." They took me to the house, and Aunt Zora put salt and turpentine on it and wrapped it up. When I look at the scars today, I realize that my guardian angel must have been hovering close that day when those saw teeth went across the top of my hand and missed all the leaders and the main blood vessels. We got on the wagon and went back to the cane mill. Mother give us a good talking to, but she didn't know how bad my hand was till one day when she went to dress it. She said my little finger ought to have been sewn up, but it healed up in a couple of weeks.

Yes, and this was the time of year Mother went to knitting. She always knitted us about three pair of hose apiece. She would send the wool away and get it carded and spun; then she would knit our hose and mittens. She always had her knitting handy. When she sat down, she would pick up her knitting.

Then about this time of year, we would put away our potatoes. People called it holing them away. Mother always holed them away between the barn and granary. It was on a ridge and the water drained away good when it was raining. She would have Arthur make a trench about four by six feet around and pile the dirt up inside the trench. Then she would level it out and put a layer of straw on it and pile the potatoes on the straw and cover them with a layer of straw and a layer of dirt. She always did this when the ground was good and dry. After we got them holed away, we made what was called a breathing hole. We would take an old bucket with the bottom out and make a hole in the dirt as big as the bucket; then we put the bucket on top of the pile of potatoes a little to the south side. She would then cover the whole business with a plank, making the roof higher on the south side. You could get out potatoes through the old bucket when you wanted some. When it got extra cold, we would stuff old sacks in the bucket. We fixed sweet potatoes the same way.

This was 1904 and my third year in school. I made friends that have lasted through the years, especially four. Their names were Mertie Austin, Mamie Moretz, Virgie Preslar, and Maude Downs. Maude was an only child, so when I went to spend the night with Maude, Mr. and Mrs. Downs would always play blindfold with us. I know we played blindfold at all the other girls' homes, but it doesn't stand out in memory like when the parents played with us. In those days, everybody carried their dinner to school. When I went to spend the night with Maude, Mrs. Downs packed lunch for me with Maude's. She had filled Maude's little basket so full the lid would hardly stay on, so we stopped when we were not out of sight of her home and ate two pieces of pie. I thought that was the best pie I had ever eaten. I remember what kind it was. It was apple custard pie flavored with nutmeg.

Each family of children carried their dinner together. We had a homemade split basket that held a peck. We didn't have waxed paper, so Mother wrapped our dinner with a white cloth and covered the basket with an Irish linen towel she had bought from an Irish peddler. One had a red border and the other had a blue border. The oldest of the family would carry the basket in the mornings, and some of the others would carry it in the evening.

At school on Friday afternoon, they would have a spelling match or tell speeches. Aunt Nora and Aunt Jina had sent us children some storybooks that had stories and poems in them. I had learned one, and I was just dying to tell it since I knew that not any of the others would have any like it. Sometimes three or four children would tell the same verse. They would get them out of their readers. Here is my public speech.

Come here to me Hen, Hen, Hen
And jump right into the big pig pen

The pig has got some good sweet corn
I gave him some this very morn

The hen flew in and pecked about
And layed an egg before she got out

The pig ate the egg and said with a sigh
There isn't any more and I wonder why

So walking up slowly when the hen wasn't looking
He ate the poor thing without even cooking

A few speckled feathers laying around
When I looked in the pen that was all that I found.

This was my first speech at school, and I will tell you my last before I finish this autobiography.

Well, spring had come again in the year 1907. School was out. We were having six months a year then. Around the turn of the century, the wheels of progress started turning. We had our first rural mail route. It came out from Taylorsville and was Route #6. Arthur had been doing the plowing since he was twelve, and since we had a mail route by the door, he wanted Mother to subscribe for the *Progressive Farmer*. She also subscribed for the *Kansas City Star* which was kind of a mixture between a magazine and a newspaper. That was our reading material. Arthur read the *Progressive Farmer* from cover to cover. He wanted to try everything new he read about and make things he saw pictured, and he could just about do it, too. He wanted to swap the mule for a big iron gray brood mare who was going to bring a colt that year. He was thirteen years old that spring, and he ran off the corn rows. Mother dropped the fertilizer; I dropped the corn, and Artie covered it, so we got along fine.

In the spring of 1906, Mother was making her year's supply of soap. Let me tell you how it was made. We saved all the ashes from the fireplace during the winter and kept them in a covered box so they did not get wet. We had an ash hopper, so I will tell you what an ash hopper is. It was made by setting up four posts about four feet apart each way, then nailing two by fours around the top to hold the posts together and the hopper in place. Then we would take a piece of 2 x 12 eighteen inches long with a groove cut all the way around about two inches from the edge. In front, it came slanting all the way to the edge of the board to make a spout for the lye to drain out. Then she took four 12-inch boards, one for between each post, and set the end of the boards in the groove in the 2 x 12 that had been made stationary at the bottom. She then nailed the boards to the 2 x 4's around the top, then fill in the corners with short pieces letting the ends come inside the first four boards put up. She then put in a layer of straw, then filled the hopper with ashes to the top, but made it lower in the middle so it would hold a bucket of water without running out around the edge. To make good strong lye, she needed to take two or three days to soak the ashes up good. Then she could put in more water and get the lye dripping to test the lye. As long as it would float an egg, it would make good soap. When she got the lye ready, she would get the big iron wash pot and fill it about half full of lye. Then she would bring out the soap grease jar which held strong edges trimmed from our homemade meat, bacon rinds, and butter that had become too strong. She would dump it all in the strong lye and start it to boiling. As it boiled down, she would add more lye till all the grease was "eat up" as she called it. Then it would begin to thicken, and she would let the fire go out. She left it in the pot till the next day. I would help carry out the stone jars to put it away in. It seemed we had stone jars or jugs to put everything in.

Let me tell you how we washed. We did not have a well, so we went to the spring to wash. We had one large homemade tub with homemade white oak bands around it. In those days, everybody had a battle bench. It was a 2 x 12 inch board with two holes bored in each end with legs stuck in the holes. Then we had a paddle made of hardwood about three inches wide and three feet long. The first thing Mother would do was make a fire around the big iron pot while I filled it with water. While the water was heating, Mother sorted the clothes. She would take the sheets and the white things that were not too dirty and put them in that old big tub with warm water and some of that lye soap. She would stir them around a little and wring them out and put them in the pot to boil. Then she would put some of our wearing clothes in the tub and here is where the battle bench came in. After I was eight years old, it was my job to battle the clothes. I would take a garment out of the tub and fold it four or five doubles along on the bench. Then I put some soap on it, paddled it with that paddle on one side, and then I turned it over on the other side and paddled it some more. Then while Mother scrubbed that garment, I would battle some more. When we finished that tub of clothes, we would empty out the tub and get fresh water from the spring. Then she would take them out of the pot and put some more in to boil. Then she would rinse out the sheets that she had boiled. I only wish that I could get my clothes washed in an automatic to look bright and clean like those sheets looked. Then she would put in the last and dirtiest tub full of wash. Here is where I really had to battle.

I have been telling you so much about work that you will think we never played, but we played a lot and had a lot of kinfolks and friends to play with. There was a steep hill back of the barn that went straight down to the river. There was about thirty feet of flat bottomland from the bottom of the hill to the river. Arthur made a homemade sled that two could ride on at a time. All the kids in the neighborhood would come on Sunday evening to ride that sled. It was a perfect place to play. It was a wooded area inside the pasture where cattle and sheep had been pastured, and there was no underbrush and the little bottom at the foot of the hill was perfect for stopping the sled. After we had ridden down the first few times, the track got slick, and it was almost like riding on ice, though not quite. Arthur found this out one icy morning when he rode down the hill. The sled shot out across that little bottom and dumped him in the river.

This is about work and play mixed. We had all the back pasture sown in small grain and would not have much pasture till after harvest, so Mother would have Artie and me take the two cows down to the river for a couple hours and let them fill while we played in the sand bar that had washed out under a huge walnut tree. One morning Artie had to help Mother hoe corn, so I took the cows alone that morning. I got real busy making a garden in our sand bar under the big walnut tree. I had set out plantains for cabbages, ragweeds for tomatoes, and crow peas for beans. I had just finished the prettiest garden I had made yet in my sand bar. I just looked up the river in time to see the cows going out of sight into a thicket of birch, red willow, opossum grape vines, and bramble briars. That bend in the river was called Beaver Bend. Several years before, the beavers had turned the river around against the hill. I always had a horror of that place, but I had to go there alone. I went about two hundred yards and found the cows standing under a big birch tree on what used to be the bank of the river before the beavers turned it. I got hold of the chains of each cow and started trying to lead them back out of that wilderness. When I got out, my feet were full of briars, my legs were scratched and bleeding, and I was still scared. That broke me from playing garden and watching cows at the same time.

In August, 1906, I gave my heart to God and joined the Fellowship Advent Christian Church; that was the best decision I have made in my seventy-three years. He says, "I will never leave thee nor forsake thee." I have found that to be true; surrender your life to your Savior while you are young. You will never regret it.

Well, spring had come again. It is 1908. We children were growing up. Arthur was eighteen; Artie was sixteen; I was fourteen; Carl was eight. Arthur had finished school, what he could get at the little one-room school. In the fall of 1907, he went to work for Mother's brother, Uncle Wiley Teague, at carpenter work. Uncle Wiley was a foreman, so he contracted and built houses when work was slack on the farm. That suited us, for Arthur could be home to help raise a crop. The peach orchard was at its best that year. Arthur took peaches to town three times a week while the main crop was in. Mother did not have to go with Arthur now unless she wanted to do some shopping. One day she had gone along. When they came home that evening, guess what was behind the wagon? They were pulling a brand new surrey. It had red wheels and a black shiny body with two seats and a top with a fringe around it. I was as happy as a little boy with his first little red wagon. Our old wagon was getting so worn with all kinds of farm work that it wasn't fit to go to church in. Now we could go in style.

Can you imagine how Hickory would look if you were dropped down in the middle of the town of Hickory and there were no cars, no paved streets, not even sidewalks? Go with me back to 1902, and you will see just that. Along in front of the stores on main drag were rocks laid for a walk. We were in town when Carl was about two and one-half years old.

This stained glass window is in the Fellowship Advent Christian Church in Bethlehem, NC. It is dedicated to Alonzo and Mary Moretz by their children.

Mother was shopping in Tom Field's Store where Katie's is located now. Mother was having Arthur fitted in shoes. She told Artie and me to look after Carl. We were standing around wide-eyed, looking at everything. The train came in, engine puffing, the smoke blowing, bell ringing, so Carl let out running down the street. When we got to looking, we could not find him. Mother was all excited. Arthur jumped up with one shoe off. He said he was going to see the train. We go to the door and sure enough about half way down the street, we saw Carl going, so Arthur with one shoe off and one on, went running down the street and caught him as he was starting to cross over to the depot. He said, "Boy, where are you going?" Carl said, "I was going down to the roc wack to see the twane." He meant rock walk to see the train. You can see there wasn't much congestion on the streets in 1902.

Dr. Henry Abernethy owned the first car in Hickory. I saw my first when I was at Grandpa Teague's. A car was going along the road about one-half mile away. It had come a shower of rain, and the red hill was slick, and they were having trouble getting up the hill, so I ran one-fourth mile to see it before they got up the hill.

Go with me back to 1905, and I will tell you some more about work and play mixed. Arthur had seen a picture of a homemade cider press in a farm paper. He got material together and made one. He set it up at the spring, so apples were always handy. So we were ready to try out the new cider press. We picked up two bushels of apples, one sweet and one sour. We washed them and put a few at a time in a big wood tub and mashed them up with a wooden maul. When we got them mashed up, we would put the press full of mashed-up apples, put the top on the press, and here is where the fun began. Arthur would take a white oak pole about twelve feet long and put it in a notch in the maple tree, then across the top of the press. Then all we kids would get on the pole and watch the cider pour. When we had filled a two-gallon jug and put it in the spring box in the house where it would stay cool, we cleaned the press and waited till we drank that jug, then we would press some more. If any got sour before we drank it, we would put it in the vinegar jug. We never wasted anything at our house.

One night about the middle of April 1903, my favorite Uncle John Moretz came to spend the night with us. Arthur wanted Uncle John to go fishing with him, so Artie and I wanted to go along. A little before sundown, we went down the steep hill behind the barn to a big rock in the bend of the river where the laurel bushes came down almost to the water's edge. Uncle John went the farthest back in the laurel beside the big rock. Arthur was next. Artie and I were huddled on the riverbank not so far in the thicket. Before dark, Arthur and Uncle John had caught three catfish and two horney heads. I caught one little catfish. It began to get dark. The frogs, owls, and whippoorwills began hollering. Artie and I were scared stiff. We were used to hearing them holler at the house, but never right in the trees above our heads where we could hear the owl's bill crack.

Uncle John knew we were scared, so he asked if we heard the birds talking to each other. He said, "Listen to them say, whip, her, will. Now listen to what the owl says, who, who." [Then Uncle John] said, "Listen to the frogs talk -- that old coarse talking fellow on the far side of the meadow. He says, Wish I'd have married when I was young, wish I'd have married when I was young. Listen to the little keen talking fellow up here on the creek bank. He is answering the old big frog. He says, Could if you would, could if you would." We forgot all about being afraid and wanted to hear the birds and frogs holler. We took our fish by the spring and put them in the big watering trough where we water the horses and left them till the next day when we ate them for dinner.

It is the spring of 1909. Our crops were all planted, and on the morning of May 10, 1909, there was a white frost that killed all the fruit and most of the crops. Especially, what crops that had been worked were killed and most of the leaves on the trees. We had a six-acre field of corn.

We had worked about two acres the evening before the frost, so it killed all that we had worked. We had to plant it over. What we had not worked turned blue and was singed at the ends of the blades, but after a shower of rain and a week's time, you could not tell it had frosted. There were peaches as big as the end of your thumb all over the ground, so we would not have any peaches to sell or apples to make cider in 1909.

A Mr. Pierce Bowman had built a new store about two or three miles down the road. Uncle Tom's children had been down there, and they came to our house all excited and said that he bought all kind of roots and herbs. They had a list of each kind with the picture of each.

They wanted us kids to go with them to dig roots. Mother said we could go the next day. Next morning, Artie, Carl, and I got our hoes to dig with and our cotton picking sacks to carry our roots in and went to Uncle Tom's. There, we were joined by Bessie, Joe, Frank, and Hattie. We decided we would just dig one kind of roots each time we went. Then we would not get them mixed up. We decided on star root because we could get more per pound for it than anything else on the list. With the list of roots and herbs, it said where you would be most likely to find each particular kind. The list said star root grew on the north hillsides in and around laurel thickets, so off we go to the old river hills below the bridge. The woods were full of kids when all seven of us got spread out looking for star roots. They were easy to dig, since they were right on top of the ground.

The next day we went, we dug golden seal. It wasn't so plentiful as star root. The third time we went, we dug bloodroot. That was the last time I saw the old river hills. In a couple days, Bessie came over and said they had found a patch of wild comfrey on Mr. Charles Simmons' place, and she had asked him if they could dig the roots. He said he wished they would dig it all. Next day we went to dig wild comfrey. We got a larger bunch of roots here than all of the others we had put together. The hardest job, and the one we got the most money from was gathering about one and one-half acres of mullein. This river hill was just covered in great big stalks of mullein. Mother said she didn't know what she was going to do with it. Then we saw in the herb list where you could get three cents a pound for dried mullein leaves. We started digging up the mullein stalks, stripping off the leaves and putting them in sacks. For the next two weeks we had the barn and granary roofs full of mullein drying.

It was a red-letter day when we took the mullein and roots to the store. We had never had a dollar of our own before. In this little country store, they didn't have many kinds of material to choose from. We wanted to get material for dresses and aprons. They just had apron gingham, dress gingham, calico, and percale. The apron gingham was eight cents a yard; the calico was five cents, and percale was fifteen cents a yard. We got material of each kind for dresses and all-over aprons and had some money left.

It was the fall of 1909. Mother was making dresses again for a group picture. Arthur and Artie had begun dating. I guess Mother wanted a picture of the brood before we began to scatter out. After the farm work was done about the middle of November, we got all dressed up in our Sunday best and climbed into that surrey with the fringe around the top and started to Hickory in style. Arthur had broken a young mule he had raised. He had worked him all summer in the field, but had not had him hitched double to the surrey many times. We got along just fine till after we had crossed the river. We were afraid that he would not want to get on the ferry, but he didn't give a bit of trouble. When we got out to the edge of the bottom, there was a small creek about eight feet across; the bridge did not have banisters, so when he got on the bridge, he began to shy away from his side till he pushed the mare off into the creek. Lucky she went down between the traces or she would have pulled the surrey in with her. Arthur jumped out and got her out of the creek, but she was muddy and dirty all over. There was a little house close by where the fellow lived that tended the ferry. We got a pan and some old rags from him and washed her off, got hitched up, and were off again for the big city. The wind had started to blow cold. Arthur unhitched the horses and tied them up on the south side of a high board fence where the sun would shine on them. We went in Hardin's Studio and had our pictures taken.

When we came to the hitching lot to go home, there was an old darkey there. He said "They are talking about prosecuting you for running your horse till you got it that wet with sweat." Arthur told him how the horse got wet. We hitched up and started for home. We got home about four o'clock, tired and hungry. We made a big fire in the kitchen fireplace. While the others did the chores, I fixed supper. I ran to the granary and got a basket of corncobs and a few onions. I piled the cobs on top of the fire and put on the skillet and lid. While they were heating, I made up my corn bread. Then I shoveled out the live coals from the burned cobs on the side of the hearth and put the hot skillet on it with a spoon of lard in it. Then I put the corn dough in and covered the skillet with the hot lid and a few shovels of hot coals on the lid. Then I got the little iron pot and

This family portrait was taken November 1909. Left to right: Artie Naomi, 17; Isma Salome, 15; Carl William, 9; Arthur Taylor, 19; and their mother Mary Louise Teague Moretz.

put a little water in it and the bowl of white beans Mother had cooked the day before and hung it on the hangers beside the fire. Then I peeled the onions I had brought in. Then I got out a bowl of dried peaches from a stone jar. They were cooked in what we called hutsels. They were little clings dried whole with the skins on and seeds in them. They sure were tasty. About this time, Mother and Artie came in from the springhouse with a big crock of sweet milk and a large pat of fresh butter, so we sat down to a supper fit for a king.

We were a healthy, happy family, and I didn't realize how soon we would be separated. I guess Mother did when she was wanting another group picture. Arthur was 19, Artie 17, I was 15, and Carl was 9. In a few weeks, Artie went to stay with Uncle Titus and Aunt Ethel. Arthur went to work for Uncle Wiley. He would always be at home on weekends. There was just Mother, Carl and me. It sure was lonesome. Spring came in 1911. Arthur came home the first of March. Mother's sister, Aunt Dovie's husband had died, so we rented her farm besides tending our own. We had two horses, and Arthur said Carl was old enough to plow. Artie came home. Aunt Ethel had got well, so she could do her work. We were a busy, happy family again. There was a hill in the pasture below the barn that had only a scatter of trees, so Arthur wanted to cut a few more of the trees and seed it in grass. Mother told him to go ahead. He and Artie sawed down the trees and sawed them up for wood. Carl and I piled up the wood and piled the brush to burn. The next day after we burned the brush, Artie and Arthur were sawing the last log up into wood, and I was piling up the little ends of brush that had not burned. One of the cows and a calf were standing side-by-side switching their tails. Arthur called to me and said, "Iss, tie their tails together," so I did. In a little bit the cow started down the hill pulling the calf by the tail. When she had gone about one hundred feet, the switch and about one inch of skin pulled off. Boys did I hate to go and tell Mother what I had done. She made me take down the stovepipe to get soot to wrap it up in. That was supposed to stop it from bleeding. Well, Arthur got the grass sowed and the crop planted. Then he went to work at the carpenter work for a few weeks till the corn needed plowing. Carl and I harrowed the whole crop. I remember I was over at Aunt Dovie's harrowing in the creek bottom. The road went along one end of the field. I saw two fellows in white shirts coming across the creek, so when I got to the other end of the field, I fooled around a while till I thought they would be past. Then I started back down the rows to the other end. When I looked up, there they were poking along so they would get to the end of the rows the same time I did. I was filled with mixed emotions. As I went down those corn rows, I was ashamed because I was harrowing, because I was dirty, and mad at them because they waited till I got to the end of the row. Yet I was glad to see them. They were going to Boone to school and were home on spring vacation. They had been to visit their brother and sister. Their names were Cloyd Trivett and Arthur Preslar.

Artie was dating Partee Bolick, so he brought his cousin Edd Flowers to date me. They each had a horse and buggy, so they took us to a lot of places that summer -- to the Fourth of July Celebration in Hickory, a big singing at the Court House in Taylorsville, and The Old Soldiers' Reunion in Newton. The summer passed quickly. When we gathered in the crop, we had a bumper crop. Arthur wanted to have a corn shucking, so he asked so many of his friends and ours that we had the corn all shucked till eight o'clock. It took till twelve o'clock for everyone to eat supper. There was a big harvest moon, and it was a warm night, so this great crowd of young people played games in the yard. Arthur had invited a boy, the brother of a girl he had dated that summer. His name was Boyd Smith. The love bug must have bitten each of us. He was nine years older than I was, so he was twenty-five and I was almost sixteen. Mother thought he was too old for me, but I thought he was it. He came two and three times a week till February, and then he wanted to get married. We had been engaged two months. He asked me to set the date, and I said October tenth. He went up in the air. He said if I cared anything about him, I would marry him then. He said I knew he was living alone trying to raise a crop. His family had moved away, and he was staying on the old home place alone. He said the girl he was dating when he met me would marry him in a minute. I said maybe he had better marry her. He went home and didn't come back for two weeks. Then he came and said he had been to see the other girl. He left that night, and I never spoke to him again. He has been dead ten or twelve years. Artie had broken up with Partee Bolick and was dating Calvin Hayes. Arthur had been dating Lola Honeycutt since early summer, and they were getting married Christmas.

I was dating Edd Flowers again. After Arthur got married, Artie went to Hickory and got a job at Elliott Hosiery Mill. Mother, Carl and I were alone again. I wasn't going to school that winter, but every two or three weeks I would go on Friday evening to the spelling match and hear their speeches. I went at dinnertime, and the teacher asked me to say a speech that evening. I said, "I don't have any." He handed me a book and said,

"Here is one." It was "The Burial of Moses." [This is part of the poem written by Cecil Frances Alexander (1818-1895.] They had classes till recess, so I read the poem three or four times and told it that evening. After all these years, I still remember it, so here it is.

THE BURIAL OF MOSES

By Nebo's lonely mountain
By the side of Jordan's wave
In the vale in the land of Moab
There lies a lonely grave.

And no man knows that
And no man saw it e're
For the angels of God up turned the sod
And laid the dead man there.

That was the grandest funeral
That ever passed on earth
But no man heard the tramping
Or saw the train go forth.

Noiseless as the daylight
Comes back when night is done
And the crimson streak
On the ocean's cheek
Goes into the great sun.

So without sound of music
Or voices of them that wept
Silently down from the mountain came
The great procession swept.

Perchance the bald old eagle
On gay bellspores height
Out of his lonely era
Witnessed the wonderful sight.

Perchance the lion stalking
Still shuns the hallowed spot
For beasts and birds have seen and heard
That which man knoweth not.

That evening when we got about two hundred feet from where the road home left the highway, we saw a man in a buggy driving a black mule. When we got home and asked Mother who he was, she was all smiles and said he was a Mr. Huffman from Catawba County. He was a veterinarian. She [Mother] had been to Luther Foxe's Auction Sale, and her brother-in-law, Uncle John Eckard, had introduced her to Mr. Huffman, and he had brought her home. He came two or three times, and they were planning to get married. Artie came home one Saturday night, and when Mother told her she was getting married, she [Artie] raised the roof. I said to her, "Listen, Arthur is already married; you are gone from home. When I find someone that I love good enough, I will marry, and then Mother would be left here with Carl alone." After we talked a while, she got reconciled to the change, so Mother began making her wedding dress. On the seventh of April 1912, they got married.

They got the license in Newton, so they had to get married in Catawba County. The first bridge across the Catawba River was above

Dr. Daniel Monroe Huffman married Mary Louise Teague Moretz on April 7, 1912. Both were widowers with grown children.

the bridge that is there now. Rev. Fate Bolick lived a little way out from the bridge on the other side, so they had him come to a little past the middle of the bridge. So they were married in Catawba County, and they were married there on the middle of the bridge. He took Mother home with him to meet his daughters, Minnie and Lottie. Minnie had been married about a month, but she and her husband had not started housekeeping yet. On Monday, Minnie said, "Now you have someone to cook and keep house, so I will move out." Her father told her that she and Lottie could divide the furniture, all but his room and the heavy furniture in the kitchen. On Tuesday, they moved out, and Mother moved in. I shall never forget how I felt that morning we left the old homeplace where I had spent so many happy hours. I felt that we looked like the children of Israel leaving Egypt. Mother and her new husband were in a two-horse wagon piled high with furniture with two cows tied behind the wagon.

Carl and I were following in the surrey with the back seats filled with clothing. I was dreading to meet my new sisters, but I didn't have anything to worry about. I liked them on first sight, and I think they liked me. I stayed with Mother until Friday, and my new Father took me up to see Artie. She was working at Elliott's Hosiery Mill and boarding with one of our old neighbor girls who was married and living on Highland Avenue. On Saturday, Calvin Hayes came to take Artie and me home. When Mother decided to get married, I promised Grandpa and Grandma Teague to stay with them that summer. We went by the old home and got the clothes I had left there, and then we went to Grandpa's. Artie stayed all night, and Aunt Ellen and Uncle Wiley came up for a while that night and begged Artie to come work for them that summer. Then she and I could be together. She went back and worked two more weeks, and then she came to Uncle Wiley's to stay. They lived next door, so we saw each other three or four times a week and were always together on

Sunday. Calvin and Edd would always come and take us to church. Then in the evening, they would take us to the old homeplace. One of our girlfriends had married and was living there. We stayed till the middle of July, and Mother begged us to come live with her. Lottie had gone to live with Minnie. She and Carl could not get along. They each were the baby; I guess that was the reason. We were living in our new home only a few days when we realized that we had to call our Mother's new husband by some name, but what? I could not say Father; I could not say Papa; so what would we call him? He was kind to us and respected our wishes. We decided to call him Daddy Huffman. Putting the Huffman to it showed he was not the only daddy we had, but [we] still respected him. We gradually dropped the Huffman, but the Daddy stuck. He has been dead twenty-nine years, and when either of us speaks of him today, we lovingly call him Daddy.

We got into the fruit drying business again. The peach orchard at the old place had about dried out, but the apple trees were at their best. Daddy would go twice a week and get a wagon load of apples, and we would dry them. One of us and Carl would always go along to help gather the apples. Daddy brought all of our dry boxes and scaffolding planks so we had something to dry the apples on. We worked hard, and when we sold the fruit that fall, we had fifteen dollars apiece – Daddy, Mother, Artie, Carl, and me.

This was October 1912, and the paper was full of ads about the first Catawba County Fair, and we were looking forward to going. The exhibits were in the old Seminary Building just behind Saint Paul's Lutheran Church. The big excitement was that an airplane was coming to

Hickory. Where Green Park School is now and all down and across the street that goes over by Howard Johnson's was in a field. That is where I saw my first airplane. They shipped it to Hickory and assembled it on the field. They had worked at it a couple of days. Before they flew it, people were standing around saying, "That thing will never leave the ground." At last it did leave the ground and flew over the circus where Howard Johnson's is and on across where the highway is and circled and came back and landed. It made three flights. Everyone went home excited. I especially, because I had made a date for the next Sunday with an old friend I had known all my life. We went to school and church together, but he had never paid any attention to me till we had moved away. I had not seen him for a couple of months when we met at the fair. We had a lot to talk about. He asked me for a date. I dated him through November, and then the first of December, I met the fellow who changed my whole life. The first Saturday in December, we wanted to go to town to do some shopping, so Carl drove us in the surrey. Daddy drove Mother in the buggy. He got there first. When we got there, he was all excited. Someone had told him his son, Arthur, had come in on the eleven o'clock train from Wyoming. He had not written that he was coming. I had seen his picture. They said he was in Wyoming, but I had never given it a thought that he would ever come home. Artie, Mother, and I were going up the street, and about where Bumbarger's is located, there stood Daddy, Ed, and Arthur. My heart skipped a beat, and I thought that is the man for me. I can still see how he looked. He was dressed in a black broadcloth suit with a light grey beaver hat standing there straight as a stick. He looked like a Philadelphia lawyer.

I guess he must have felt the same way about me. He told his brother, Ed, as they came home talking about Artie and me, the biggest one was his. He didn't come here to stay till the middle of January. He was boarding at Billie Pitts'. He would come over three or four nights a week. The whole family would sit by the big fireplace in the kitchen till bedtime. Daddy and Mother would go to bed. Artie, Arthur, and I would sit and yack till the fire burned down. I was still dating Arthur Preslar. The last night he was there, I think we were all miserable. I wanted to be with Arthur Huffman, and he wanted to be with me. Arthur Preslar was caught in the middle through no fault of his own. It started raining, and he left early. Arthur Huffman said to himself when he heard him leave, "He will not come here anymore if I can help it."

Next morning I went to milk, and he went to feed the horses. He was in the cutting room. I was in the cow stable. He handed me a bucket of meal for the cow. When I handed him the bucket, he took my hand in both of his and held it tight while he said, "I want you to decide till tonight which one you love the best, Arthur Preslar or me." I was in the clouds all day, for I knew what he was going to ask me. We could hardly wait for the others to go to bed that night so we could talk. The first thing he said was, "Have you decided what I asked you this morning?"

I said, "I decided that the first time I saw you." He then proceeded to ask me to marry him, and I said I would. He was the only man for me. Then he asked when we could get married.

He said, "You know I am a minute man. Let's not make a big to do about it. What about next Sunday?"

I said, "I can't get a dress ready that soon."

He said, “Wear some of those nice dresses you have, and I will see that you get something nice later.” So we decided on the next Sunday.

Sunday morning I went with the family to Fellowship Church. There was a funeral that day. It made us late getting home, and we were late getting dinner. Arthur came in and said, “There was a funeral over there, and there is going to be a wedding over here if you don’t object.” That was the first anyone knew that we were getting married.

Now I will tell you how I was dressed. I know you will want to know. What all the young set was wearing that winter was navy or black skirts with white blouses. I had a navy skirt and white blouse. The blouses were made so you could wear different collars. I thought my collar was too big. Artie had a small lace collar, so I put it on. She always kidded me about starting to work in double harness with her collar on.

We were married in the parlor at home. Artie’s boyfriend, Arthur Starnes, and Gretta Miller, a friend, were witnesses. Rev. J. D. Mauney performed the ceremony, Sunday, February 9, 1913. We have lived happily ever after.

This portrait celebrates Isma and Arthur's wedding on February 9, 1913.

Generation Two

For Christmas 1972, Isma Salome Moretz Huffman published an expanded edition of Memories Dedicated to My Grandchildren. This book includes the Generation One material plus memories of her life from the time of her marriage to Arthur William Huffman on February 9, 1913, to her 76th year.

Dear Grandchildren,

I am writing some memories of the second generation in my lifetime that I hope will be of interest to you.

I hardly know how to start to finish the autobiography I started in "Memories of the First Generation." I know you will pardon if I repeat myself getting started. When you have had a good marriage like I know I have had, I don't think you can tell it too many times.

It was a sunny, balmy evening on the ninth of February, nineteen and thirteen. Arthur and I were married at four o'clock in the afternoon. You ask where we went on our honeymoon. One of my girlfriends, Gretta Miller, was there, and she stayed till it was getting dusk. So Arthur and I went with her part way home. We were married at Grandpa Huffman's old place. The road we went walking home with Gretta went slanting out to where you cross the creek. Then the way you go in Hal's drive to their riding ring, then it went slanting down the hill across the cotton field to the big creek. Then [we went] through the woods up to her home. We walked back alone. I guess you could call that a honeymoon, for there was a full moon shining down, and he kissed me at least half a dozen times going home. We didn't go on any trip till 25 years later when the baby in our family was 14 years old. I will tell you about that trip later.

We just went to work on Monday morning like we always have. Arthur had rented the old Thorton place. He was to fence it for the rent two years. So he started to build the fence Monday morning. He worked at the fence till Wednesday night.

He had brought some broncos when he came from Wyoming. He had swapped the last of the broncos for a big, black stallion. He heard someone wanted a stallion over about the three state corners of Tennessee, West Virginia, and North Carolina. So Thursday morning, he left riding Tamarack and leading the stallion. He thought he would be home Monday.

Sunday Uncle Titus and Aunt Ethel came to see us. Aunt Ethel said, "Here is the bride. Where is the groom?" I laughingly said, "He has left me," and from the look on their faces, I think they thought he had, but a thing like that never crossed my mind.

Monday evening we ate supper, and I put his supper in the oven to keep warm. I was all ears listening for the horses' hooves. He had come and unsaddled Tamarack, and I heard him hanging up his saddle. I opened the door. He said, "Isma." We met about halfway between the house and barn. I threw my arms around his neck with his around my waist. He turned round and round till he came to the well box. Then he sat me down, took my face between his hands and turned it up toward the full moon and said, "Let me get a good look at you." Then arm in arm we laughing went into the house. The ecstasy of those moments will stay in my memories as long as I live.

While Daddy and Arthur talked horse trading, I set out his supper on the kitchen table where we could sit by the big fireplace and talk. Daddy asked us to stay with them and help farm that summer. We were glad to stay. Arthur finished his fence [and] then went to plowing to put in a crop.

There are four Arthurs in our family. I will give you their names so you will know who they are when I speak of them -- my husband, Arthur Huffman; my sister's husband, Arthur Starnes; my brother, Arthur Moretz; and my brother-in-law, Arthur Yount. When we would have a family gathering, we would always get a snapshot of the Arthurs in the family. Those pictures are precious because they have all passed away, except my husband, Arthur Huffman. It makes us realize that time is passing, and we are passing with time. The best each of us can do [is] in the words of the poem "Thanatopsis" by William Cullen Bryant:

> "So live, that when thy summons comes to join
> The innumerable caravan which moves
> To that mysterious realm, where each shall take
> His chamber in the silent halls of death,
> Thou go not, like the quarry-slave at night,
> Scourged to his dungeon, but, sustained and soothed
> By an unfaltering trust, approach thy grave
> Like one who wraps the drapery of his couch
> About him, and lies down to pleasant dreams."

Through the months of March and April, Daddy and Arthur were busy plowing, getting ready to plant a crop. Mother and I were making quilts and embroidering pillow cases and scarfs to have ready when we moved in our own home.

It was so cold in June 1913. We had to wear our coats while we were cutting and bundling wheat. We were working on that hill where Hal's house stands. We sure kept busy that summer. We raised a lot of vegetables to can, made jellies and jams, canned berries and apples and peaches, raised Irish and sweet potatoes, pumpkins, [and] butter beans for dry beans. I had made pickles and relishes. Arthur had bought and raised a hog that summer, so we had things like we each had been used to when we were ready to move to ourselves.

The first house we lived in was Henry Clontz's old house. It was a new house then. We rented it from Quince Smith. We were expecting our first baby the thirteenth of November, and we wanted to get moved before it was born. Artie, my sister, was going to stay with me. We had all of our furniture moved in and were going to move our clothing and vegetables and canned goods on Saturday. I had them all packed and ready, but Saturday morning I was sick and vomiting all day, and at twelve o'clock Saturday night, November 1, 1913, Clifton was born. He weighed just five pounds. I breast fed all my children. Cliff was little when he was born, but after the first month, he grew like a little pig. Guess I was like a little Jersey cow the way Cliff grew.

We moved to our first home November 15, 1913. We didn't have much furniture, but I sure was happy trying to fix up what we had – trying to make it look homey.

Arthur bought seventeen acres of land from Daddy. It was the lower end of Revis' place joining Hal. We had aimed to build on the hill above Hal's dog lot, but we got a chance to buy the place we live now. So we sold the 17 acres to Quince Smith.

On March the 15th, we rented the old Poley Hahn place, one hundred and twenty-five acres. You children will remember it as the Tuttle place. The old house (now North State Academy) has been torn down. It was a large two-story house with seven rooms, three halls and three porches. My little furniture was lost in that big house. Arthur still had a lease on the Thorton place. He bought some calves and pastured them that summer. He hired Dewy Hartsoe, a fifteen-year-old boy, to help with the farm work. I helped haul cotton and corn. I would take Cliff along and set him in a box under a tree at the edge of the field. We had all that big field on the side of the road as you go to White Cross laundry planted in cotton.

We had ten acres planted in corn in the river bottom. We would go to the field in the wagon, take our dinner along, and stay all day. There was a one-room log house at the edge of the bottom. We would put Cliff close to the door so he could see out. We got Aunt Davie's daughter, who was 10 years old, to stay with Cliff whiled I hoed corn in the bottom. Her name was Viola. When she grew up, she married Sheriff Ray Pitts.

It would always take us three days to work the bottom corn if it didn't rain and get the ground too wet. We had a garden and a lot of corn planted around the house.

When we moved here, we sure had good neighbors. The Frank Poovey's and Rufus Hatley's were our closest friends. Mary Hatley and

Jane Poovey were just like a mother to me. I was young, and they gave me a lot of good advice. They showed and told me how to do a lot of things.

I shall always remember Ascension Day, 1914. I had got up bright and early, finished with breakfast, and had made a large turn of light dough to make bread for dinner and enough for several days. Mr. Rufus Hatley came to the door and said, "Mary says for you and Arthur to bring that baby and come down for dinner." I said, "I wish I could, but I have just made a large turn of light dough and have to stay and bake my bread." He went home. In about half an hour, Mrs. Hatley came up in the backyard where I was drawing a bucket of water from the well and said, "You go in the house and get this chicken to cook. You wouldn't come eat with me, so I am going to eat with you. Maggie is picking some strawberries." In a little while, Maggie came with a gallon of strawberries. We capped them and put sugar over them to soak. I made out my light bread. While the bread was rising and the chicken was cooking, we had a little break. Maggie said, "Let's eat on the back porch." There was a wide shady porch on the north side of the kitchen, so we moved the table out there.

I opened a couple cans of green beans, fixed a cooker of rice, and made cream chicken. We had strawberries and cream for dessert, [and] then hot rolls and coffee. Maggie and I were joking while we were fixing the table on the porch. We were like kids. She was 14, and I was 19. I said, "Who is going to ask the blessing?" Up to this time, we were doing what my little namesake, Amanda Isma Huffman, calls "pigging."

One day I told Amanda people who didn't thank the Lord before they eat were like a pig under an acorn tree—always receiving God's blessings and never looking up to thank Him. One day when she was eating dinner with us, she and Grandpa had sat down before I sat down. And he hadn't asked the blessing. She looked up and said, "Grandma, we are 'a pigging'."

I guess Mrs. Hatley was sitting on the porch listening to Maggie and me joking so when we sat down to dinner, Mrs. Hatley said the nicest blessing. I felt so little the way we had been joking. Mrs. Hatley has been dead fifty years, and I remember the blessing plain as if it had been yesterday.

Here it is: "Dear Lord, we thank Thee for Thy gifts received through Thy bountiful goodness. Pardon all our sins and save us for Christ's sake."

The Bible says, " . . . they shall rest from their labors and their works do follow them." How true that has been of Mrs. Hatley. When I remember her through the years, I always think of the blessing she said that day in 1914. We don't have to make a big, flowery speech to be remembered. We just need to say the right thing at the right time that will help someone.

We had worked hard that summer and had raised a fine crop. We got the crop all gathered in and wheat and oats sowed till about November 15.

Then Arthur made an agreement with Bob Colts, the man who owned the farm we were living on, to cut a lot of hickory trees for wagon spokes. He got a neighbor, Mr. Avery Davidson, to help saw the trees, and they went halves in what they made. Mrs. Davidson and I made quilts. Mrs. Hatley, Mrs. Jane Poovey, and my mother helped. We made a quilt at each one of our homes and three at my home. I needed to make more. I enjoyed the fellowshipping with them. They are some of my most pleasant memories.

Well, let us retrace our step and go back to July, 1914. That is when my sister, Artie, left to go to Montana to meet her true love, Arthur Starnes. She arrived at Great Falls, Montana, and they were married July 26, 1914.

In August, Arthur brought his Grandmother Huffman, who was in her early nineties, to stay a few days with us and Grandma Poovey. Grandma Poovey wasn't our Grandma, but that was what we always called her. She came over and spent the day with us while Grandma Huffman was here. She was in her nineties also. Her name was Emeline. Grandma Huffman's name was Rhoda. It was a real treat to me to hear them tell about coming to the woods as brides riding horseback, where they each still live. They told about their husbands going off to war and about the Yankees coming through and taking their mule and leaving them an old, poor, tired mule, but when they fed it and got it rested up, it was a younger better mule than [the one]they [the Yankees] took. They told about putting their homemade meat in a wooden box and burying it in the cornfield and plowing over it to hide it from the Yankees.

I have always loved old people. Some of the closest friends I have had through the years have been older people. I pray I can stay lovable and be of some service to humanity what years I have left.

Well, March 1914 [1915 is compatible with the birth of Mary Mae] rolled around, and Arthur started another crop. He hired Duke Younce, a fifteen-year-old boy, to help farm that summer. I was pregnant, so I couldn't help much the first part of the summer. He [Arthur] had rented the Thornton place again that year besides the farm we lived on. Sometime in January, I. J. Keller and his wife, Mary, died about three weeks apart. They didn't have any children. So the County Commissioner sold their home, and we bought it. It was the land we are living on now. We bought it the second day of May, 1914.

On May 10, 1915, our second child, a baby girl was born, weight 9 pounds. Dr. Gamewell Flowers was our doctor. He said we had 2 weeks to decide on a name. I told Arthur I would decide on the first name, and he could give her the last name.

Arthur and Duke went to plant corn on the Thornton place the next day. They had taken their dinner along, and while they ate their dinner, they named the baby. I had told Arthur I wanted her first name to be Mary after my mother. So they decided that her last name should be after a month. She was born in May, so they called her Mary Mae. That night at the supper table Duke said, "We have named the baby." Arthur proudly told what they had decided on while they ate dinner.

When Mary Mae was three weeks old, we hitched up to the buggy, and I went along to the field to drop peas in the corn before they plowed it. We put the buggy under a large walnut tree about the middle of the field. We put Mary Mae in the buggy bed, and Clifton played under the tree what time he wasn't trying to follow Arthur, Duke, or me. They were each plowing corn, and I was dropping peas between the hills of corn. You see, one of us was passing by the buggy every few minutes. Cliff got a big kick out of following after us. He thought he was farming. When he got tired, he would lay down under the walnut tree and go to sleep. He was just eighteen months old.

There were about six acres in the field we planted in peas. There was ½ acre of creek bottom that people who always lived on that old farm used for their garden, and it was real fertile soil. So we planted it in corn and cornfield beans. Talk about beans, we had them! Never before or since have I seen so many beans on one piece of ground. We canned all we needed and gave to the neighbors and picked 3 or 4 sacks of dry and green mixed before it frosted. We didn't have Mexican beetles in those days.

There were about five acres of river bottom on this old Thornton farm. It wouldn't grow anything but watermelons. So we planted two acres of melons. This was the last year we worked the Thornton place.

I had worked all over the farm, but the river bottom. I had never been there. It was about the middle of June, and this was the last time they would work the melon vines. The vines were three to four feet long. We had to lay the vines around straight with the rows. Then scatter a few peas over the ground. Then plow the melon vines and then straighten them out. It was a slow particular job. I went along to help that day.

You say, what could I do to help with two children, one 20 months and one two months old? Like the old saying is, "We went prepared." We always went in the wagon, and this time we parked it under a large mulberry tree. We left Mary Mae in the wagon and turned Clifton loose with a large collie dog. Everywhere Cliff went, that collie was at his side. If he sat down, the collie would lay down not three feet away.

We always took our dinner with us when we worked in the river bottom. You wonder what we had for dinner. I always fixed dinner while I fixed breakfast. I made enough biscuits for dinner when I made the breakfast biscuits. While they were yet hot, I would wrap them in a paper bag and tie them shut. They were good and fresh at dinner. I would roll out a crust from a piece of that biscuit dough and make an egg pie. I would use 2 eggs, 1 cup sugar, 3 cups milk, a heaping tablespoon flour, and a teaspoon vanilla. I poured this mixture in the crust and baked it while we ate breakfast. Then I would take a one pound can salmon, 2 eggs, 2 cold biscuits crumbed fine and a dash of salt [and mixed together]; then I made patties and browned on both sides in bacon drippings. You know back in those days we could buy three one-pound cans of salmon for a quarter. Then I would put about a quart of quartered Irish potatoes in an iron pot so they would cook quick. I would put a tablespoon of butter, teaspoon salt, dash pepper, and when they boiled dry, I would pour in a cup of sweet cream, let come to a boil, and take out in dish and cover. They were really good at dinner with some spring onions. We had some hardboiled eggs, and this was our menu at our picnic at the river bottom under the mulberry tree. I guess there is sixty feet of water standing where we ate our dinner that day. [In 1927, Oxford Dam was built on the Catawba River, and Lake Hickory was full pool in 1928.]

After all the crops were gathered in November 1915, we moved to our own home where we still live although not in the same house. Arthur told me when we moved in the old house, "Live in this fifteen years, and I will build you a new one." I didn't dream I would live that long in the old house, but it was exactly fifteen years.

The first night after we moved, the neighbors serenaded us with shotguns, circle saws, and cowbells. There were the Pooveys, the Smiths, the Hatleys, the Davidsons, and the Hartsoes. After they had gone around the house 2 or 3 times, we opened the doors and invited them in and served them apples, good soft pears, and peanuts, roasted and still warm.

We were still neighbors just living a little farther away. We sure did enjoy the serenade of those dear people. I can shut my eyes and see them and hear all the kind words they were saying. I still know their grandchildren and great grandchildren. I have one for a dear daughter-in-law. [Jeanette Baker Huffman, wife of Forest Huffman, is the granddaughter of Avery and Leona Davidson.]

We were living in our own home now, nothing fancy, but it was home. There were five rooms and three porches and a good basement under the main part of the house. [There was] a good well, a granary built of logs, a corncrib and a barn with wider sheds built around it.

We had about a dozen old apple and peach trees and one pear tree. The first thing Arthur did was set out twelve peach trees and six apple trees. One of the apple trees is still living after fifty years. It's named Summer Queen. We built a garden fence, set out a strawberry patch, plowed the garden, planted onions and lettuce, and set our cabbage plants before Christmas.

This is the cover of Isma's 1972 memoir that she distributed to her family for Christmas. Daughter Mary Mae did the line drawing of the old home where they lived for fifteen years before building their two-story craftsman style home in 1927-28.

The first of the year Arthur was busy building a fence for a larger pasture. We always kept two milk cows, so we would never be without milk.

While he was plowing for the spring crop, I was setting out flowers and shrubs and making a hot bed to raise tomato and pepper plants to sell. We also had setting hens to raise a lot of chickens. We had Buff Orpingtons, a big yellow almost gold chicken.

I guess you think by now we were really heathens because I haven't said anything about church. We had gone three Sundays out of each month since we had been married. Arthur was a Lutheran, and I was an Advent Christian. There were preaching services at Mt. Olive [Lutheran Church] twice a month, and there were services at Fellowship [Advent Christian Church] once a month, and we attended both. We didn't attend Sunday School at either place.

We visited all our kinfolks and friends on the fourth Sunday. I have some real happy memories of visits with my aunts and uncles. They have all passed away but two -- my mother's sister, Aunt Lola Teague and Aunt Ethel Moretz, Uncle Titus' wife.

It was the summer of 1916, our first year in our own house. We had nice crops growing in the creek bottoms where the lake is now. On Thursday evening about the middle of July, it began to rain, and it never stopped till Saturday night. Sunday morning when we got up, all we could see of our corn was the tassels sticking up above the water. It looked like the lake looks now, only out in the middle it looked like it was rolling and boiling. You could see floating along different things from buildings to stacks of straw. It was a sad time for farmers who were depending on creek and river bottoms for their corn. There just wasn't any left. Our corn was covered in mud and the corn shoots just stopped growing.

It [the severe storm] washed the [Highway 127] steel bridge off its piers. It was a bridge just like the one that is there now only it was not as long. It just had to cross the river. The lake didn't back up till 1928. We had to cross the river on a ferry till they built the new bridge.

As 1917 rolled around, Arthur got wanderlust. He wanted to sell our livestock and go to Wyoming. I wasn't sold on the idea, but I was like Ruth and Naomi, "whither thou goest, I will go."

We didn't sell our home. We just aimed to stay out there till we saved enough to pay for the place. I got busy sewing for Cliff and Mary Mae and for myself enough to last us for a couple years. I intended to work when I got out there and would not have time to sew. Mostly house dresses is what I made for myself. I made one nice black wool serge dress for traveling.

Mother had bought an Edison phonograph that winter, and there was a record where a lady sang, " I want a hat with cherries, with big squeshy [squishy] berries." I guess that song must have affected the hat styles that spring. When I went to buy a hat, all the better hats were full of cherries.

I had never traveled any, and I thought I had to dress up. I should have bought a couple of nice scarves. I needed a hat like a dog needs Sunday, as we will find out later.

This stunning photograph of Isma with hat is not the infamous hat that she took to Wyoming. However, it is easy to see why Arthur Huffman fell in love with this beautiful young woman.

I bought a fancy black straw turban with a large bunch of cherries on the top edge of the crown behind coming down the left side to just above the eyes. It was a pretty hat and looked nice on me, but who needs a hat riding on a train!

Arthur was busy getting the farm in shape to leave it so the land would not wash. He had all the field above the house seeded in small grain, so he seeded the field below the house in spring oats and red clover. Daddy was going to look after having the grain harvested.

Arthur got all the buildings in good repair. He bought 2 large trunks, 2 suitcases, and 2 overnight bags. We filled the largest trunk with bedding and the others with our clothing.

On March the tenth, 1917, we were all ready to go to Wyoming. I was dressed in my black serge dress with my frilly black straw hat trimmed with cherries.

We had not traveled far before I realized that I needed to take off my hat and lay it above our seats with our bags. I didn't have it on again until we changed stations in Chicago. We left Hickory at eleven thirty a.m., and we got to Knoxville, Tennessee, about dark. Arthur's sister, Oma, was at the station. The train wasn't leaving till ten o'clock. We went out to her home for a short visit.

We didn't have to change trains till we got to Chicago. We didn't only change trains; we had to change stations. We had to ride in station wagons from one terminal to the other. The wagons were pulled by two gray horses. Their feet went clop, clop on the pavement. That taken Cliff's time. He said, "They have awfully pretty horses out here and mighty fine wagons." The next couple of days we saw some mighty pretty farming country through Illinois, Iowa, and Eastern Nebraska. In Western Nebraska, we were snowbound for three hours.

One evening it looked like it was snowing, but the sun was shining. The wind just picked up fine, dry snow and sifted it around. It had drifted on the track till we were in snow up to the windows. We were between Chadron and Old Port. They sent a snowplow from Old Port to clear the track. We got to Casper, Wyoming on Friday night at twelve o'clock and could not find a place to sleep. We had to stay in the depot. We weren't the only ones. It was full of people. We got to Riverton, Wyoming, Saturday about four o'clock.

Arthur got us a room and the first decent meal we had since we left Hickory. He looked up John Miller who was loading two wagons with supplies for the summer. Arthur was going to drive one wagon, and the children and I were going along and stay a few days while Arthur looked for work. Arthur wanted me to stay in Riverton till Monday morning and go up to Miller's on the stage that carried the mail.

Mr. Miller said, "You are welcome to ride on the wagon of supplies, but it is sixty miles to Lander which is the nearest place you could get a bed to sleep. I expect we will camp on the prairie." That didn't scare me. I was still like Ruth and Naomi, "whither thou goest I will go and whither thou lodgest I will lodge."

Mr. Miller had large wagons with wide, high beds with four horses to each wagon. They were really piled high with supplies. We opened our trunk and got out a blanket and quilt. I climbed in the middle of the wagon bed, and Arthur handed me Mary Mae and Cliff. I wrapped the blanket around our feet and across our laps and [wrapped] the quilt around our bodies. We were very comfortable, but before the day was over, it got tiresome.

Well, the sun was getting low in the west. Crowheart Butte looked as far away as it had in the morning. Then we knew it was sixty miles away. Mr. Miller said, "the first time we come to a big enough place where the snow has blowed off the ground, we had better camp." In a little while we came to a place where the snow had blown away, so he drove the wagons up side by side about 10 feet apart. Then he took the big tarpaulin off the top of the wagons and fastened it to one side the wagon bed then down on the ground between the wagons and up the other wagon bed.

We opened our trunk and took out all our quilts and blankets. Mr. Miller had a sleeping bag, so he got along fine. He took the tarpaulin off the other wagon and put it on top of our bedding, and we got along o.k.

He made a fire with sagebrush and melted snow for water and cooked corn meal mush and seasoned it with butter. He made coffee that tasted mighty good. We ate canned sausages with the hot mush. We all slept with our clothes on, and I pulled off my shoes. I thought it would rest my feet. It would have been all right if I had put them in bed with me, but I didn't. By morning they were frozen so hard I could hardly get them on.

We got all our bedding put away, and I got my hat with the cherries out of the trunk where it had stayed for the night, while we were using the quilts. I wish I could have left it in the trunk, but we had a hard time getting the bedding back, so if I wanted to keep the hat, I had to wear it. You can imagine what that looked like setting high on that load of supplies, wrapped in a quilt wearing a fancy hat full of cherries.

We had been traveling about two hours when the stage caught up with us, and you bet I was glad to get on. There was just one passenger and the mail carrier. We got to Lander about twelve o'clock. We stopped to exchange mail and eat dinner. There was just one woman that kept the Post Office and fed the mail carrier and the people who were on the stage coach. She got gone a little while we were eating. I didn't know where she had gone. When she came back, there was another woman with her. She just stood around and watched the children and me. It made me feel kindly silly.

It was about ten miles up to Mr. Miller's, so we crossed Big Wind River. We came to an Indian Village. There were dozens of teepees and squaws walking around with their blankets on and papooses on their backs. That took Cliff and Mary Mae's time, and I guess I was wide-eyed too. That was the first real Indians I'd ever seen.

The mail carrier saw we were kindly carried away. He said, "Everybody who comes on the reservation has to wear a blanket like a squaw." He said Mrs. Miller and Geretto wore blankets (that was Cloyd Miller's wife and sister he was speaking of). About three o'clock, we came in sight of the Miller ranch. That was the second house I had seen since I left Riverton. Of course there were several houses in the town of Lander.

I sure was glad to see Sarah. She came up the driveway to meet me. Geretto was teaching school across the river. She came home, and it was good to see old friends.

Cloyd and Sarah were moving to their new home. They finished moving the day Arthur and John got home from Riverton. Their home was about four miles up the river from John's.

Arthur got a saddle horse from John and went looking for work. He came back on Monday. He had work with a Scotchman, Charlie Sauter, as foreman of his ranch. I was to do the cooking. His wife had died. He had one little girl. She was six years old, and her name was Jessie. His wife's sister, Mae Phife, took care of the little girl. Mr. and Mrs. Phife, his father and mother-in-law lived with him also. That made five in their family and four in ours -- Nine in the family besides three hired men. All the time he was a big sheep man, and every two or three days Miss Phife would come to the door and say two extra for dinner or three extra for the night.

Men would be coming off the range for supplies or bringing wool. You never knew when you would have an extra, so you had to be prepared.

They had two dining rooms, one for their family and one for the hired help.

While I was cooking a meal, I would set the table in the hired help dining room. Then I would dish out the food for the family and put it in a serving cart. Miss Phife would come get it and serve the family. After the meal was over, she would bring the dirty dishes back on the cart.

I sure had a lot of dishes to do.

Would you like to know what we ate for breakfast? We ate oats for cereal, pancakes and butter, syrup and fried eggs. For dinner our meat was mostly beef, but sometimes a leg of lamb or chicken. We always had potatoes, and I baked yeast bread.

My recipe – 3 medium potatoes cooked good and done, mashed and whipped till no lumps left. Pour in one half-gallon water, a heaping tablespoon salt, three tablespoons sugar, and 2 cakes compressed yeast. Stir in one quart flour to make a thin batter. Put in a warm place in a large container and let stand overnight. In the morning, add enough flour to make a pretty stiff dough. Put it out on a floured board and knead it till it is smooth and elastic. Then put into a greased container and let rise about two hours. Then make out in loaves. Let rise till double in bulk. Bake. When nice and brown, take out of oven and grease top with butter. Wrap and put in your breadbox.

This is the recipe I used to make all that bread in Wyoming. I don't go to all that trouble now. When that bread was baking and warm, you could smell it all over the place. It sure made me hungry to smell it.

Now I will tell you about the part of the house that was my responsibility. We will talk about the kitchen first. That is where I stayed most of the time. There was a large Majestic range that burned coal. I don't think it ever got cold the three months I was there. There was a large worktable with a shelf underneath to keep all the pots and pans.

A door was on the outside wall with a glass to let in light with a window all the way across above the stove. The other side was the door to the family dining room. Open shelves were across the rest of the room to store staples that we used every day such as coffee, baking powder, rice, [and] salt, to name just a few. There was a slat across the bottom of each shelf to keep things from falling out. If you put things in right, you could glance over it and see everything you had, which beats looking through a cabinet. The hired help dining room had a long table that would seat ten people, with two windows and a door at the side opposite the kitchen. The rest of the furniture was ten chairs, a high chair for Mary Mae, an icebox, and a breadbox. The breadbox was metal lined. When you put those yeast loaves in that breadbox, they stayed fresh two or three days. There was a pantry off the outside of the dining room where they kept heavy groceries such as flour, meal, sugar, salt, rice, beans, [and] all kind of canned goods.

We had two small rooms we slept in. That was the part of the house that I looked after.

I had to wash the towels from the bunkhouse that the hired men used and the dishtowels from the kitchen besides doing the washing for my family.

Arthur did the milking, and I took care of the milk. Let me tell you what kind of a milk house they had. Right behind the house, there was a little hill [and] they had dug back in the hill and made a room about 8 x 10 feet and covered it with plank. Then they had placed a whole mountain of dirt over the top and a heavy door at the front side to go in at. They had a long table to set the milk pans on and tin pot lids to cover them. When I washed those milk pans, it made me think of the poem, "the row of shining milk pans sunning in the fresh sweet breeze." [Grandma Isma is quoting from the poem "The Old Farm" by George H. Maxwell. The poem appeared in *Green's Fruit Grower and Home Companion*, November 1907.]

Beside the milk house was the icehouse, made just like the milk house only larger. They cut blocks of ice out of the river in the winter and filled the icehouse. Then they had ice to use all summer.

There is one more thing I want to tell you about. It was the vegetable cellar. It looked like a little mountain on the outside. It was about 10 feet by 20 feet. I never saw such a pile of potatoes before or since. They had carrots, turnips, onions, cabbage, [and] winter squash.

One evening I was doing my ironing and watching Cliff and Mary Mae out the dining room window. They were playing on top of the little hill beside the milk cellar. All at once, they were gone. I put down my ironing and ran to the hill [and] away down through the prairie. They were going hand in hand. Each one had a handful of pink flowers. I could not bring myself to scold them for if they had not gone out in the prairie, I would never have had all those pretty wild flowers. We went down to the irrigation ditch and walked back to the house.

When we got about one hundred feet below the bunkhouse, we saw a pretty little animal. It was black with white stripes down its back. It was on the far side of the ditch. We could not get close to it. Arthur said we should be thankful we could not, or we would have been like "the young man from the city, who saw what he thought was a kitty. He gave it a pat and ran after that. He buried his clothes, what a pity." [Grandpa Arthur was quoting a limerick that appeared in a 1906 book titled *Limerick Lyrics: A Collection of Choice Humorous Versifications* selected by Stanton Vaughn.]

One afternoon, Arthur was going to Lander for supplies about twenty-five miles away. His team was traveling along pretty fast. Cliff's little red sweater was just so far behind going just as fast, and I was so far behind it wasn't funny. After a while, I let out a yell that Arthur heard, and [he] looked back and saw what was following him. He let Cliff catch up and talked to him a little and spanked him a little and went back down the road. It was a lot farther going back. Mary Mae was still asleep, thank the Lord.

It was May, and it snowed most every night about an inch [and] sometimes two, but by noon it was all melted and gone. As soon as the sun came out, it began dripping off the house. People called it the May wet snows.

Arthur and I had been talking and planning what was the best thing for us to do. I was pregnant. If I stayed out there, we would have to rent a house, and it would take all he made for us to live on, and we could not save anything that way.

Miss Phife begged me to stay two or three months longer, but we were afraid if I stayed that long, I would not be able to travel that far alone with the children. So we decided for the children and me to come back to North Carolina and stay in our home, and Arthur would stay out there the rest of the summer and the next till we saved enough to pay for our place. That was the hardest decision for me to make in my whole life.

My sister, Artie, lived in Conrad, Montana. She begged me to come up there and she would take care of me, but she lived out on a homestead sixty miles from a doctor.

On June the fifth, 1917, Cliff, Mary Mae and I left Riverton, Wyoming, for Hickory, North Carolina. The kids held on to their Daddy's neck till the train started to pull out. I didn't have a chance. I can still see him standing there on the platform. It was hard knowing it would be eighteen months till I saw him again. He stood there as long as we could see him.

I don't remember seeing so many things as I went back to North Carolina as I did going out because I had two children to look after all by myself.

I remembered seeing such large apple orchards as we went through western Iowa. As we went out, the trees were dormant. As I came back, they were in full leaf.

On the second evening, I got a terrible headache, so I took a sleeper that night. I would get in Chicago the next morning. Cliff and Mary Mae got a good night's sleep. Although I didn't sleep much, I at least got to stretch out my legs.

When we left Riverton, I could not buy a through ticket – just to Chicago. When I got to Chicago, I asked to buy a ticket to Hickory, North Carolina. They said they didn't sell tickets to Hickory. I would have to be transferred to another terminal. I guess they thought I knew what to do, but I didn't in that busy terminal. I was frightened. I had to hold on to Cliff and Mary Mae. If they got away for a minute, they would be swallowed up in the crowd.

I saw a policeman. He was real nice. He helped me get my ticket to the next terminal and check my baggage and helped us get on the right wagon to take us to the terminal. We got there and got our ticket and started on our way again. When I realized I was hungry, we had eaten all the things we had brought with us and had just been living on the little knick-knacks they brought through the train. The train stopped, and the conductor said they would be stopped one half hour. A lot of men were getting off, and I asked one nice looking fellow if he would get us some sandwiches. I told him I wanted ham and lettuce and some kind of fruit pie, [and] some milk for the kids. They didn't have pie, so he got jellyrolls. People are nice when they see you need help.

We had to wait two hours in Cincinnati and two hours in Asheville, but the biggest treat I had on the trip was somewhere in the mountains between here and Asheville. The train stopped to get water. An old man came along the window of the train with a great big platter of warm, fried chicken, with warm fried bread to eat it with. That was the first warm food I had had in four days.

We got to Hickory around six o'clock. I called home. Daddy was out on a call to see a sick cow. I was in Setzer's and Russel's Drug Store phoning home. Their drug boy was just getting ready to leave to go down to the college. They said we could ride down to Willie Hollar's and spend the night with Lottie.

Next morning Daddy came and got us. The kids were sure glad to get where they could play.

I just got home in time to bind six acres of rye in that field over next to the camp. My brother, Carl, cut it when he was just seventeen. Daddy got Clinard Poovey to cut the wheat with a binder.

Clinard rented all the land on the other side of the creek to sow in small grain. The field above the house Arthur had seeded in red clover before he went to Wyoming.

Mother didn't want me to move to our home till after the baby was born. We had our own wheat for bread, and I helped buy what we had to buy. I did all the cooking, so Mother could work in the field and garden. I wrote to Arthur once or twice a week and prayed for him every day. I was like Daniel praying with his face toward Jerusalem. Seemed I could pray better with my face to the West. My prayer was, "Lord, he is out there under these great starry heavens somewhere. Watch over him and protect him and bring him safely back to me and help him to understand thy Word."

I bought one dozen young hens from Mother to raise to lay eggs for us next summer. Artie promised to come next summer and stay with me. I bought a nice Jersey heifer to make a cow till I moved back home.

The children stayed well. I didn't have to write Arthur and say they were sick.

There were a lot of apples and peaches on the place. I canned a lot of fruit and vegetables to have that winter.

On November twenty-fourth, 1917, our third child was born, a boy weighing nine pounds. When I wrote and asked Arthur what he wanted to name him, he said, "Name him anything you want to just so he will bring me a drink of water quick when I want it." Arthur's name was Arthur William so I named the baby Allen William.

His Daddy wasn't here to spoil him, but his Grandpa was. From the time he was a month old, his eyes would follow his Grandpa around the room when he came in till Grandpa would bend over the crib and speak to him. Then, he would pick him up and go over by the fireplace at the window and talk to him and hold him for an hour or more. I think that was the reason Allen always was Grandpa's pick of the boys when they grew up, and I think he was closer to Allen. He was always doing little things for Grandpa. I didn't think much about it then, but as I grow older, I realize what it meant to Grandpa.

Now I am going to tell you about what the "everyday down to earth people" in the whole country were doing to make a few extra dollars. So many of my friends after reading my other book of memories ["Generation One"] said why didn't you tell them about stringing tobacco pokes? Back then you got your cigarette and pipe tobacco in little cloth bags, with drawstrings at the top to hold them shut. Putting those drawstrings in is what they called stringing pokes. They came packed in heavy duck sacks. They were hemmed at the top, and the side seams were sewed with yards and yards of them together. You had to clip them apart [and] then slip them over a little crooked wire and turn them right side out. Then with a darning needle, you would put a heavy flat string two double through the hem, cut [the strings] off leaving 3 inches, [and] then tie a knot in the end of two strings tying them together. Then you pack them up and tack them together, twenty-five in a pack. You did this all for a dollar and a half a thousand. Mother and I made forty dollars a piece that winter stringing pokes. There was so much snow you could not get out. There was snow on the ground for six weeks. There were thirteen snows on top of each other. One day about the middle of February, it rained, hailed, sleeted, snowed, and thundered with lightning all in one evening.

Cliff and Mary Mae played out in the snow all winter. They would come in with hands just blue. They were so cold, but they never had a sniffle all winter.

Well, it was April the first, 1918, and I was getting ready to move home. Artie was coming the middle of May to spend the summer with me. I wanted to get the house cleaned and moved in before she got there.

Every day or two, I cleaned the walls, and I washed the windows and floors. Arthur had left an old leather jacket hanging in the dining room. As I would pass by it, I would kiss the sleeve and brush away a few tears and think it won't be as long as it has been till he will be home again. I got everything cleaned up, and the middle of April, I moved in. It was terribly lonesome, but I knew it would not be long till Artie came. She had a little girl, Charlotte, three years old, and she was expecting in August.

I got busy and planted a large garden, so we would have plenty of vegetables to eat and can.

My young hens were laying all the eggs we needed to eat, and I was setting every one that would set. I bought two fine O. I. C. pigs. [These are white, pedigreed pigs that grow to a very large size. The organization of O. I. C. Swine Breeder's Association was located in Ohio at this time.] I got them from Uncle Wiley Teague. When they brought the pigs over, he said, "If you want them to grow, put them in that red clover in the garden." So I put them in. They did fine. By the last of the summer, they were great big hogs. It came a rainy spell, and they turned that garden upside down. That has been fifty years ago, and that part of the garden is still hard.

One day the last of April, Cliff came running to the house and said, "We have a little calf down in the pasture." Cliff was sure proud of that calf. I told him that now we would have plenty of butter and milk, eggs, chickens, fresh vegetables and fruit. We could live at home and board at the same place.

The third Sunday in May, Artie and Charlotte arrived from Montana. It wasn't so lonesome any more. It was haymaking time. The five acres above the house was in red clover. Grandpa cut the clover, and Mr. Cook, a neighbor who lived where Mrs. Nance lives now, hauled it to the big shed at the back of the barn. I helped fork all that hay. After Mr. Clinard Poovey harvested the wheat across the creek, he said he would plant those fields in peas. If I would pick them and furnish one-half the fertilizer, he would furnish the seed, work them, and thresh them. So we had twenty-eight bushels for each of us when he threshed that winter.

On August the tenth, Artie gave birth to her second child, a boy she named Dayton. He was crying for a few nights, and I was up rocking him. Artie said that a baby would be natured like the one who carried him outside first. I said, "Here goes. He is going to get better or worse - one or the other." So I picked him up and carried him around the house. I couldn't tell any difference.

Artie and the baby did fine. Artie's husband, Arthur Starnes and Arthur Huffman would each have a new baby boy to see when they came that fall.

September was here, and the peas were getting ripe, and I was picking every day. Cliff was just five, but he was a good nurse for Allen. He would sit in the foot of the cradle and put his feet out through the spokes till Allen went to sleep. Then he would get out of the cradle and play with Mary Mae and Charlotte. He acted like a little Mama to all the kids.

One day Artie said she wanted to go along and help pick peas. Grandpa Starnes had brought an old timey cradle for her to use for the baby. It was light so we carried it along and set it under a big apple tree just above where the road goes into the camp. Mary Mae and Charlotte wanted to go along. There was a huge walnut tree below the apple tree where we set the cradle with Dayton in it. We told them to play under the walnut tree. They had played good for an hour or two, and we heard Dayton crying. We looked and Charlotte and Mary Mae were up at the cradle trying to rock him. When Artie got there, they had stripped off ragweed blossoms and poured his face full. He had them in his mouth, nose, and eyes. After that, Artie decided she had rather stay at the house. Those girls were always into something! One day Artie caught them trying to wash Allen's head. They were lathering it with octagon soap.

The first of October, Artie took the new baby over to see its Grandpa Starnes. I had about a third of the peas to pick yet. There was a long porch on the side of the house facing the lake, only it was just a creek then. Cliff wanted me to move the cradle out on the porch so he could see me all the time I was picking peas. Every little while, he would call to me, and I would answer him. That way he didn't get too lonesome. He was always a dependable child, and he sure tended Allen well. He would rock him to sleep in the cradle and sit for hours in his little rocking chair and rock and sing to him. He looked after Mary Mae too. He was like an old hen looking after her chicks instead of a five-year-old boy.

November had come, and Artie and I were each looking for our Arthur's. Hers came first about the third of November, and they had gone over to his father's. On the tenth of November, 1918, Arthur came home. I have told you how nice he looked the first time I saw him. That was nothing to compare with how nice he looked that night! He had on a dark suit with a dark red, light weight cashmere slipover sweater with a tan wide brimmed Stetson hat. He was thirty years old, some hundred and eighty pounds, six feet tall with a ruddy complexion from working in the outdoors. He sure was a Prince Charming to me when he came up in the yard that night. He said, "Isma," just like he did five years ago when he came home from selling that big stallion. I was in the yard almost till he got it said. He lifted me off the ground, and that is another kiss I'll never forget.

We went in the house to see Cliff and Mary Mae that he hadn't seen for eighteen months and Allen, a year-old son he had never seen. He had to start all over getting acquainted with his family again.

Next morning, you should have seen Cliff taking his Daddy around showing him the cow and calf and the two nice big hogs, we had ready to butcher. He even went to show him the nice clover hay we had in the barn. He threw out some grain to the chickens so his Daddy could see them. The rest of the year Arthur spent cleaning up around the place, cutting wood for the winter and stove wood for next summer.

1919, first of the year came. He bought a team of horses and began to plow for a crop. He also bought six cows and a cream separator. You would milk the cows and while the milk was yet warm, you would strain it into the reservoir on the side of the separator. You would turn a crank and the milk would go through the machine and the cream would come out at one spout and the milk at another. We had a heavy five-gallon can with a tight fitting lid and handles on each side to let the cream run into. It set on the porch in the winter. We took it to the basement in the summer, and we would churn twice a week and deliver butter to customers in town.

I had not gotten to church but two or three times while Arthur was away, so we went twice a month when warm weather came. Cliff and Mary Mae would sit on a plank across the buggy bed set facing us leaning against the dashboard. Arthur, Allen, and I would sit on the seat. It sure was a buggy full.

The summer of 1919 passed quickly, and on October the twenty-third, our fourth child, a baby boy, was born weighing eight and one-half pounds. When Arthur brought Allen to see the baby, he [Allen] cried like his little heart would break.

After I got able to do the work, he [Allen] would go to Cliff when he got tired and sleepy and say, "Rock Clitty rock, rock Clitty rock." Cliff had taken care of him so much he felt like he was his Mama.

Allen asked why we called him "Jim" till he was nearly grown. Just after World War I, there was a hit record everybody was playing on their phonographs about an old colored woman's son coming back from the war. You could hear her son singing in the distance and she was saying, "I hear him, dats him, dats him, dats my Jim." So when Allen would say "rock Clitty rock," and we wanted to talk petty to him we would say, "I hear him, dats him, dats my Jim." It was a petty name, but it was about to stick to him till he was grown.

Oh, I forgot to tell you what we named the new baby. This was the third boy, and I thought it was time we named him after my father. So we named him McCoy Alonzo. The Alonzo is after my father. With six in the family, we could hardly get into a single buggy any more, so Arthur got us a Mountain Hack. It looked just like a buggy, only it had two seats and was heavier built. He got it from Mr. Pet Tuttle who had moved down here from the mountains. His children were all grown, and he didn't need it any more. We had a way to go to church now without being crowded so much.

Nineteen and twenty one, we received the hardest knock of our married life, or we thought so at the time, but later we knew it was a blessing in disguise. Along the first of June, Arthur got a bad spell of dysentery. He was real sick for a week and not able to work for three weeks. McCoy took sick when Arthur was sick for a week, and I was sick all the time I was pregnant.

After Arthur got able to be up, I went to the cotton patch. The grass was taking possession of our crop. We had that field over next to the camp planted in cotton. Mr. Avery Davidson had that field above the line fence planted in cotton, and [there was] just one of me on our side of the fence. I was like the old colored man saying, "one n----- and one row sure went slow." When we would come out to the end of the rows at the line fence, the Davidsons and I would always talk a while and joke about [there] just being one on my side of the fence. There was a power line running from Icard's dam to Shuford cotton mill that crossed through the middle of our field. I joked and told them when it got too hot, I could just reach up with my hoe and touch the power line.

Along the last of June, Arthur had gotten able to plow, and we had the crop all worked out nice. We had the nicest tomatoes we had ever raised with just a few beginning to turn. Then one evening about two o'clock, we heard a hard clap of thunder. We hadn't noticed there was a cloud coming up back in the southwest. There was a high, slim cloud just ready to cover the sun. In ten minutes, it looked like it was a fog cloud rolling along the ground with a yellowish cast at each side. Arthur said, "There is hail in that cloud." Sure enough, we stood hand in hand looking out the window and saw our summer work being beaten into the ground. The tomatoes that looked so nice one hour ago were all full of holes. The cotton stalks looked like they had been trimmed up. We had paid $75.00 for fertilizer for our cotton, and we didn't get but one bale of cotton that fall. There were just a few bolls that got ripe. It was just full of bloom at frost. That was the last year we tried to raise cotton.

In September, Arthur got a job in the furniture factory, and the children and I did the farming. Instead of raising cotton, we raised everything we ate. We always raised garden vegetables enough to eat and can and some extra to sell. Arthur would deliver them in town as he went to work mornings. Arthur made money for our clothes, taxes, school, church and extra to seed grass till he had gotten the whole farm seeded to grass.

On January 19, 1922, our fifth child, a baby boy, Forest Wiedron, was born weighing 12 pounds. He was the biggest baby in the family. Dr. Stevenson was the doctor. Cliff and Mary Mae were going to school. The schoolhouse was where Ransom Miller's house is now. Its name was Fairview. They had to walk to school.

I started to school this summer too -- not to learn from books, but to learn how to do man's work on the farm. Arthur had a job in the furniture factory in town, so the farming was left to Cliff, Mary Mae, and me. Arthur always helped evenings after work.

Mary Mae looked after Forest, McCoy, and Allen, and [she] cleaned the house when she was only ten years old. I would plow, and Cliff would

This is a photograph of the employees at Hickory Chair Company in 1935. Arthur is the ninth person from the left on the second row. His son Cliff is the second person from the left on the third row.

hoe. Arthur would plow till night when he got home, and I would help Cliff. Allen would bring us a drink of water to the field.

So you see the whole family worked together in summer. The only time the family got to be all together was on Sundays, and morning and evening meals, and from supper till bed time. We made good use of those hours. Some of the happiest hours of my life were at meal times when the children were growing up.

The spring of 1923, we decided to cut a yard of timber and build a new house. We were all excited.

Over where Allen's house stands, we had 2 acres of old field pines. They were so big they looked like forest pines. We cut them and all the other timber we had on the place. Arthur quit his job for a couple of months and got a neighbor boy, Ross Huffman, to help cut the timber.

He got Mr. John Poovey to set up his sawmill in between where the road goes up to Allen's. He could drag the logs right down the hill to the mill. He hauled the lumber and packed it up below the road in front of the house and let it dry a couple of years. That summer after the crop was laid by, Arthur went back to work in town. Cliff and I had the job of working up the tree laps into stove wood. Arthur got Mr. Dave Eckard to come with his power saw and saw it in stove wood length. Cliff and I split it up ready for the stove. There was a lot more than we would use till it would rot, so every week Cliff would take a load to town and sell it. He was just eleven years old. We had a gentle horse. His name was Brownie, and there weren't many cars on the road those days.

Cliff was so small people along the road would tease him and say, "Hey boy, whose Daddy are you?" He would say he was Arthur Huffman's Daddy.

The summer of 1924, Uncle Arthur Starnes, Aunt Artie, Charlotte, Dayton, and Kenneth came back from Montana to stay. They came in July. Artie went to work in the paper box factory, and they stayed with us. That made twelve in the family.

That was the hardest winter I ever spent. There were five in school and three at home. I packed light lunches every day for Cliff, Mary Mae, Allen, Charlotte, and Dayton for school and the two Arthur's and Artie for work. Then I had McCoy, Forest, and Kenneth and myself at home. There was breakfast to get early for work and school. The children had to walk then. I always cooked a good warm supper for the dozen of us. Then all those dishes were to wash. Of course Artie helped with the dishes at night, but my biggest job was doing the washing and ironing. I had to draw water from the well in a big iron wash pot and scrub them by hand. I always washed on Tuesday, and it took all day. There were five beds to keep clean. Everyone wore long handles and blue jeans. It was like doing a washing just washing the socks for that crowd by hand!

I have told you some of the hardships. Now I will tell you of the joys we had. Artie, my only sister, had been living in Montana for ten years. It took us eight months to get caught up on our talking, and it was a treat for Mary Mae to have a girl to play with. All the cousins that came to visit were boys.

Arthur and Artie had a car, so they took us visiting and to church. The First Advent Christian Church in Hickory was built in Longview in 1924. The first services in the new church were in September. Arthur [Huffman] joined the church that week.

I had prayed for ten years that he would join. That is some of the joy I was talking about earlier. Not just at the time, but through the last half-century we have enjoyed working together for the Lord.

The spring of 1925, Arthur, Artie and the children moved to Arthur's father's, Mr. Pinkney Starnes, to help him farm that summer. I have a lot of pleasant memories of Artie's children that I wouldn't have had if they hadn't spent that winter with us. I especially remember Dayton preaching. There wasn't any church near the homestead in Montana where they lived, so he hadn't been to church till he came here. He would get up on the steps or a chair and wave his hands and say everything the preacher had said and then some.

Sometime in May 1926, we bought our first car. It was a 1926 Model T Ford. Now we had a way to get to church, and we have been there every Sunday since when we are able. Having a way to get to church and take part in the services has helped me to have a richer, fuller life than I could ever have had without it, and it helped [me] to raise a Christian family.

I had not been to any towns, but Hickory, Newton and Taylorsville before we got the car -- only riding on the train to Wyoming and back. We sure did enjoy the car as a family. That summer we went to all the church meetings there were in the conference. We went to Lenoir, Collettsville, Tabernacle and Boone that first summer.

We would pack lunch and have a picnic. Cliff was thirteen, Mary Mae was eleven, Allen was eight, McCoy six, Forest four. The children were all getting old enough to help with the work and take responsibility. Each one had his own job, and he was responsible to see that it was done. Cliff looked after feeding and bedding down all the stock. Allen did the milking, McCoy got in the wood, Forest filled the reservoir, [and] Mary helped with supper.

Supper was the happiest meal of the day. Arthur was home, and we didn't have to hurry. Each one could tell of the happenings of the day that interested them, and we enjoyed ourselves. There were four boys sitting on the bench at the back of the table. You can imagine there was always plenty to tell. There was a lot of hard work for everyone and a lot of precious memories, especially for me. I guess there are for the rest of the family, too. [Sometimes] I hear them and their cousins and friends talking about the good times they had at our house when they were growing up.

The children were all going to school but Forest the fall of 1927. I had learned to do all the [horse] team work on a small North Carolina farm. I am going to tell you about the job I got the biggest thrill doing of any I remember. It was October 10, 1927. There was a cool wind blowing out of the northwest. It would pick up the yellow leaves of the hickory and poplar trees and carry them across the field here above the house where I was drilling wheat. The ground was in perfect shape, not a rock or clod

Isma was six months pregnant with my father, Hal Huffman, when she drilled the wheat on that lovely October day in 1927. Pictured here at age 8 months, Hal was born on January 5, 1928.

to be seen. I had a new drill and a good team of horses. You children will remember Brownie and Robby. They would step out good and lively. All I had to do was sit up on the drill and drive the team and stop every little while and put fertilizer and wheat in the drill. Arthur had hauled the wheat before he went to work and put it where it would be easy to get.

All of 1927 we were looking at houses trying to decide what kind of house we wanted or could afford. We decided what we wanted and made our own plans and let the contract in April.

As soon as it got warm enough so we didn't have to have fire, we began tearing down the old house. We tore down three rooms and moved to the kitchen and one bedroom for Dad, Mary Mae, Hal and me to sleep in. We cleaned out the brooder house and the boys slept in it that summer. We had the new house done, and we moved in the last of September.

It seems there were a lot of things happening in 1927 and 1928. Duke Power Company had built a dam 12 miles down the river and [Lake Hickory] started to fill up the first of 1928. It began to back up in Huffman Cove the last of March and by August it was about full.

The boys caused me to almost have a nervous breakdown before they all learned to swim.

I am getting a little ahead of myself because on January fifth, 1928, a nine-pound boy was born to the Huffman family. We were all crazy about him. It had been six years since there had been a baby around our house. We named him Hal Franklin. He was the last born in the old house before we tore it down.

He had it kindly rough that summer. There was a large apple tree above where the old house stands. We used that for a living room. Every day we would carry Hal's cradle up under the tree. The sun had a way of moving around, and a lot of times, I would get busy and forget to move him. He would get a sunburned nose and cheeks. We had a grand time that summer even if we did nearly live outdoors. A lot of our friends would come evenings, and we would sit in the grass in the backyard or around the edge of the old kitchen porch and talk and have good fellowship till bedtime. I have some pleasant memories of those days. The last of July 1928, Arthur's brother George, his wife and two sons Emit and Clyde came in from Oregon. He hadn't been here since he went to Texas when he was 21. Grandpa had a big reunion. All the kinfolks and friends for miles around came. We all enjoyed it. That was the last time we saw them. George and Jinnie are dead, Clyde died in his twenties, and Emit was in Guam the last I heard from him.

In July 1929, Arthur's brother, Tom, his wife Julia, [and their] children Bruce and Catherine came in from Wilcox, Arizona. He hadn't been home in twenty-five years.

We had another reunion and big picnic dinner. That was the last time we saw Tom and Julia. Bruce and Catherine are still living in Wilcox, Arizona.

We were enjoying company since we were in the new house and had a place to entertain. We sure did have company. Hardly a weekend passed that we didn't have company, either us or the children. I think I enjoyed the children's company as much as they did.

Arthur and Isma built this home in 1927-1928. The oak tree at the edge of the yard still stands today in 2021.

We will go back to 1925. A lot of people were going into the chicken business. Arthur said that we would just grow into it and learn the business as we went along. That year we raised 56 purebred Barred Rock hens, and I built a chicken house 20 x 50 feet; the next spring we bought a three hundred egg incubator and started in February to hatching chickens. It was my job to turn the eggs twice a day and watch the temperature because I was always here. When winter came, we had three hundred pullets to put in the laying house.

They had been up about three weeks and had just begun laying when one night somebody stole forty. It makes you feel mighty bad when you have worked as hard as I had to get them raised to let it pass.

After two years we sold the Barred Rocks and got White Leghorns. We kept two to three hundred till the panic in the early thirties when we sold eggs for nine cents a dozen. We quit raising chickens [and kept] only a few for home use.

The spring of 1931, I thought I would try raising turkeys. I bought two settings of eggs and hatched 23 turkeys. They only grew till they were the size of half grown chicks when they all died but four. I decided to use them for our Thanksgiving supper for the church. The Mission Society sponsored it, and we had it at our house. I made up a little rhyme about what we would have to eat, and they printed it on the tickets. Here it is:

The WHFM is giving a Supper
At the hospitable home of Arthur Huffman.
We will serve turkey with dressing, lettuce and tomatoes,
Also stringed beans and candied potatoes.

For dessert, pumpkin pie the best you've seen
Baked nice and brown and topped with whipped cream.
Hot rolls and coffee, you won't mind the expense
You get all of this for just fifty cents.

Come when you like you will be served any time
As the hands of the clock go from five up to nine.

Children for you we are making a cut,
When [We] know if you are hungry you can't eat so much,

You will have just like the others, not such a large bunch,
So twenty-five cents you can pay for your lunch.

Isma Huffman's Sunday School class, circa 1952. Isma is the first person on the left in the middle row.

Mary Mae had a knack for fixing things, so she decorated the tables for the dining room. She took a huge pumpkin, cut the top out and scraped the pulp out and used it for a Horn of Plenty. [She] filled it with vegetables and fruits and set it on a bed of autumn leaves in the middle of the table with candles on either side. We had card tables set up in the living room, and the den, and Hal's and my bedroom. Everyone was through eating by eight o'clock. We sent out a lot of plates. The women of the Mission Society of the church furnished all the food and helped with the cooking and serving it. We had a lot of good fellowship and made money for the Society also, but to me the greatest blessing was the memories I have of those days and of the dear ones that have passed away that were here then. They are Aunt Davie Propst, Aunt Oma Eckard, Mother Clarissa Poovey, Carrie Teague, and Davie Teague. There are a lot of other members passed away since then, but these were members of the Circle. I hope to have lived so that my memories will be sweet to those who are left behind.

Well, 1932 is the year the family started to break up. On January 16, 1932, Cliff got married. He was just 18 and Jennie [Lineberger] was 16. I thought they were just children, and I guess they were in ages, but Cliff had taken the responsibility of a man since he was eight years old, and Jennie had been raised on a farm to work by good parents. So they grew together and got along fine. Instead of losing a son, I just gained a daughter. They have raised us as fine a family of children as you can find in the country.

That just left five children at home. Mary Mae, 17; Allen 15; McCoy, 13; Forest, 11; Hal, 4; and Millie wasn't born yet.

In the early thirties, the panic was so bad the place where Dad worked went broke. He was out of a job for almost a year before he found work. People were walking the streets begging for work. We were in better shape than people who lived in the city for we did have most of our food. Everything we could, we raised on the farm. Mary Mae had a job at Whisnant Hoisery Mill. She furnished all the money the family had for a year or more.

Mary Mae Huffman, 1935

Arthur planted a lot of vegetables that summer. He didn't have work. He would take a load of vegetables to town. What he didn't sell, he would give to our friends that he knew were out of work and didn't have a garden.

Arthur had been out looking for work all day and hadn't found anything. Next morning, he was going across the bridge to the fields on the other side of the lake. He had been praying as he walked. He said, "Lord, I have always worked for a living, and I want to work now, so I am asking you to help me." While we were at the dinner table that day, a man came after him to go work, and he hasn't been out of work since when he was able to work.

The fall of 1934 I was left alone. The boys were all in school. It was Hal's first year and Allen's last year. Allen didn't have to have but 2 units to graduate, so he just went till dinnertime and then came home. That way, I didn't have to be alone but four hours out of the day. I was expecting the last of December.

On December 31, 1934, our last child was born -- a baby girl weighing seven and one half pounds. We named her Millie Kate. She didn't stay a baby long. There were too many grownups to handle her. She was walking when she was eight months old and climbing like a squirrel upon everything in the house.

In 1935, Allen graduated from high school and went to work at Hollar's Hosiery Mill. Arthur told him, "We don't want to make a penny off you. You can give us a small amount for board, if you are going to save your money. But if you are not, you can pay us just like you would have to pay a stranger." That's the way we treated all the boys. [They] didn't have any trouble with the board, and all saved their money.

In August 1936, Arthur, Hal, Millie, and me took four days vacation, the first we had taken since we had been married. We went to Blowing Rock Camp Meeting. We sure did enjoy ourselves.

McCoy and Forest built the lower rock wall between the house and the lake while we were gone. They were just finishing it when we got home. There was an old Mr. Moore from South Carolina up at Camp, and he rode this far with us on his way home and spent the night with us. He could not get over the boys building that wall while we were gone. I didn't think much of it at the time, but when I think back, I realize that was a pretty special thing for the boys to do.

McCoy is seated holding Millie Kate. Standing are Forest and Hal. Photograph is taken in front yard of Huffman Cove home, 1935.

In 1936, we swapped our '26 Ford for a '36 Chevrolet. We didn't go much, only to church, but we always went Sunday morning and night and Wednesday night. The boys had it Sunday afternoon, Tuesday, Friday, and Saturday. Allen and McCoy were courting pretty heavy, and Forest was just coming sixteen. Mary Mae got it once in a great while. So you see, one car would hardly go around for this family, but we made out.

In 1937, Forest finished high school and went to work in Brown's Hosiery Mill. Now there were three boys, Mary Mae, and Dad all working in different places and going in the same car.

The winter of 1938, Grandpa Huffman [Daniel Huffman] took sick. One of the boys stayed every night all winter through February, and the first of March, someone had to stay up with him all night. Arthur, Allen, McCoy, [and] Forest took it turn about staying half a night at a time. The first of April, Grandpa got able to be up and about but not able to do any work. We tended his crop that summer.

Grandpa said that fall he didn't want them [Grandma Mary and him] to spend another winter alone. Arthur told him we would be glad for them to move in with us. If he got sick, we could care for him much easier. We had a much warmer house than they did, so the first of November they moved in with us. We gave Cliff our den furniture and let Grandpa and Grandma use the den for their room. It was the warmest room in the house. It was heated by a coal heater.

Our family stayed in the kitchen most of the time. Then the kitchen was 14' x 18', so we had plenty of room. The bathroom has been taken off the end of the kitchen since then.

Of course with two families living under one roof, there had to be some adjustment, and I think everyone did just wonderful. I remember how the boys, when they would come home from work evenings, would go to the den and joke with Grandpa awhile before they did anything else. When they came in at night when they had been courting, they would come quietly in the kitchen, pull off their shoes, and tip toe through the hall and up the stairs so they would not wake Grandpa and Grandma.

1939 was the coldest winter it had been since the lake backed up in 1928. In'39 the lake froze all the way across solid. People came from town to skate on the lake. Allen made a sled that could ride one at a time. He put car bumpers on the runners so it would run fast, and they would go down the hill and across the lake in thirteen seconds starting at the big hickory tree below the garage.

Such a cold winter! It was a good thing Grandpa did move in with us. He was not bad sick like he was the winter before, but he wasn't able to be up but about half the time. Summer came, and he sat out under the oaks [for] most of the time he was up. We would close the doors and let him sleep till nine or ten o'clock.

On Saturday morning, August 3, 1940, the rest of the family had gotten up early. I wanted to can corn while the boys were there to help. The boys had gathered it [the corn] while I got breakfast, and we had two canners full on the outdoor furnace at eight o'clock.

Grandma came out on the back porch and said, "Come in here." As soon as I looked at Grandpa, I knew he was dead. He had not been well all summer, but his death was unexpected.

Mary Moretz Huffman with her adult children, circa 1938. Seated: Mary's father, Elijah Teague; Mary's second husband, Daniel Huffman; and Mary Teague Moretz Huffman. Standing left to right: Arthur Moretz and wife, Lola; Carl Moretz and wife, Vervey; Arthur Starnes, husband to Artie Moretz Starnes; and Arthur Huffman, husband to Isma Moretz Huffman.

The funeral was conducted at Mt. Olive Lutheran Church. Ministers taking part were Rev. N. W. Harrison, Rev. Alton Trivett, Rev. W. O. Sigmon, [and] Rev. F. W. Bradshaw. Interment was at Mt. Olive Church Cemetery at 3 o'clock Sunday evening August 4, 1940.

Before Grandpa moved in with us, he deeded his place to us. The deed said if he passed away before a year, we should give Arthur's brothers and sisters fifty dollars a piece. If he lived a year, we weren't to give them anything. He just lived eight months. Arthur gave them $125 apiece.

We had to cut the place up and sell it to pay doctor bills, funeral expenses, and the heirs. We sold what was Grandpa's land on this side of the lake with three acres of our place to Allen to get enough to pay doctor bills and funeral expenses. Grandma [Mary] bought the house and five acres of land for $1,400. It took one thousand dollars to pay the heirs, [plus] one hundred and twenty-five for a monument. We had $300 and seven acres of land, and we still had Grandma to care for and furnish a house for as long as she lived.

This is when our family started to scatter. On December 7, 1940, McCoy married Louise Huffman [no relation]. McCoy and Louise got married at her church by her pastor. Charles Ray Yount [a first cousin] and Francis got married in South Carolina the same day. McCoy had bought a little Ford, so they all went together and witnessed at the other's marriage. McCoy and Louise rented a little house between Springs Rd. and the Old Newton Highway. They had it furnished before they got married, so they just came home.

On February the third at eight o'clock in the morning 1941, Allen and Evelyn [Austin] were married in Mt. Olive Lutheran Church by her pastor. They went to Jacksonville, Florida, on their honeymoon.

They stayed with us till they built their little house [on 29th avenue in Hickory]. They moved in it February the first, 1942.

In 1942, the boys started going into the service. Forest was the first. He joined the Air Force on October 17, 1942. It seemed that everyone who wasn't going in the service was going off to defense work. Cliff was gone to Florida to work in the Navy yards. Arthur and McCoy were at

Arthur, Isma, and Granny Mary, circa 1948.

Williamsburg, Virginia, working at defense work. Mary Mae was working in Charlotte. Grandmother [Mary] was staying with Jenny and the children while Cliff was away on defense work. That left just Hal, Millie and me to hold the fort. It sure was lonesome.

Hal was fourteen and Millie eight. I will never forget the first night after Arthur left. Hal brought the shotgun upstairs and put it in the holder above his bed and a large butcher knife in the window. He said, "If anyone tries to bother us, I will give them a hard time." I guess he felt the responsibility as the man of the house. He did look after the cows and horses like a man. He was in high school, Millie was in grammar school, and I was alone.

Christmas 1942. Left to right: Isma, Jerry, Cliff, Allen, McCoy, Granny Mary (on porch), and Forest in his Air Force uniform.

I sure had a treat for Christmas when the whole family was home for a few days. Forest had his first leave after six weeks service. We had just three grandchildren then: Lorene, Horace, and Jerry. It snowed the night before Christmas. I never will forget what Horace sang all day Christmas day. Here it is:

> "Over the hills and through the woods,
> To Grandmother's house we go,
> The horse knows the way to carry the sleigh
> Through the white and drifting snow."

That was our first family gathering after part had left home, and it was our last till the war was over. In a few days, all went back to their jobs, and Hal, Millie, and I were left alone again.

About the middle of February, there came a windstorm that blew about one fourth of the shingles off the north side of the house. Hal hunted up what wasn't torn apart, and he and Allen put them back on the first evening. He brought shingles the next evening, and they worked till dark, but they didn't get done that night. It rained that night till I had every bucket, cooler, and pan catching water.

This photograph of the home place taken in 1943 shows the missing shingles from the windstorm Isma describes.

On March 15, 1943, Arthur came home, but he wasn't able to work. He had sciatica rheumatism in his hip and leg. He put Hal to plowing the pasture hill with a hillside plow. They got it in good shape and sowed it in spring oats and pasture grass. By the middle of April, Arthur's legs were so bad he could not walk without crutches. Hal and I planted and tended the crop. Millie cleaned the house and looked after Dad. He tried three or four doctors here in Hickory. He didn't get any better.

He went to Granite Falls twice a week for six weeks to see Dr. Copening. He wasn't any better till a friend, a Mr. Hahn, told him about an old home remedy. Dad took it for two weeks. By that time he was able to beat up rocks in the driveway to improve [prove] it [that he was better]. In case you might want to try it sometime, I will give you the recipe:

2 tablespoons Epsom salts
2 teaspoons baking soda
2 teaspoons cream of tartar

Mix these ingredients, then take one teaspoon one-half hour before breakfast with juice of one half lemon.

On August 4, 1942, Allen's first child was born, a boy. They named him Allen Jr. On March 16, 1944, Allen went into the service. He went to Ft. Leonard Wood, Missouri, for his basic training. Then [he went] to Jefferson Barracks at St. Louis for the rest of the time he was in the service. He came home June 23, 1946.

On September 8, 1942, McCoy's first child was born, a girl. They named her Barbara. On June 23, 1944, McCoy went into the service. He joined the Navy and went to Camp Perry at Williamsburg, Va. He served in Japan. He came home from the service March 1, 1946. Louise and Barbara stayed with us while McCoy was overseas.

On January 7, 1946, Hal went in the service in Germany in the Occupation Forces. After he had his basic training, he had a weekend pass. He came through Charlotte, and Mary Mae came home with him. It was eleven o'clock when they got to Hickory. They came out to the house on the twelve o'clock bus. Mary said when Hal got off the bus and started down the road, he began to yodel, and in five minutes his two rabbit hounds were there jumping all over him and licking his face. Hal was the last one to go into the service and the last one to get out.

Forest came home November 17, 1945, after twelve hundred hours in the air as a radio operator. Forest was the first to go into the service and the first to get home.

I sure was glad to see him come home. With four boys in the service, it took a lot of praying, but I always had the feeling that they would get back. I've always been thankful that they did.

The first thing Hal did when he got home was to dig and build a cesspool for a bathroom. Our kitchen was 18' x 14' so we took off 8 feet for a bathroom. We sure have enjoyed the use of the bathroom.

Forest and Hal were busy these days looking for wives. So on June the fifth, [1948] Forest was married to Jeanette Baker at four o'clock in the afternoon at Mt. Olive Lutheran Church. They went to Myrtle Beach on their honeymoon. They came home to an apartment on the Old Newton Highway.

In '48, the wedding bells were ringing around Huffman's Cove. On July 17, 1948, Hal and Rachel Berry were married at Connelly Springs Baptist Church. They went to Blowing Rock on their honeymoon and came back to their own little home in Windy City.

Now our family was back to four – Arthur, Mother, Millie, and me. Since the boys were gone and Dad wasn't able to do the heavy farm work,

Happy to be home from WWII, four of Isma's sons happily resume the tradition of Sunday lunch on Huffman's Cove. Left to right: Allen, Jr., Allen, Forest, Hal, and McCoy, circa 1947.

he built a fishing dock. Hal had helped him build a little drink stand before he went into the service. They had anchored it up at the bridge. The water was too shallow there, so [they] moved it later.

He [Arthur] just sold drinks, candy, crackers, and fish bait and [he] had half a dozen boats to rent. He just opened evenings after people got home from work.

The spring of '46, he built a new pier to put the drink stand on and built four more piers and fastened them together with heavy coils [of wire]. He set the pier with the drink stand on it out front about 30 feet from the bank with a walkway from the bank to the pier. He put lights all along the bank of the lake and out in the [drink] stand and along the middle of the pier with seats built all around the outside of the piers for people to sit while they fished.

Someone had to stay at the pier all the time, so Dad sowed all the farm to grass and kept a few cattle to keep the grass eaten down.

I kept house, tended a large garden, milked a couple of cows, [and] raised a large flock of chickens each year.

One day sometime the first of August 1946, Rev. R. L. Isbell, Rev. Dwight Banks, a missionary on furlough, and Rev. Richard Polk came here to see if Arthur knew any place they could have a Youth Camp.

Arthur told them that if they could buy that wooded couple of acres from Everette Bowman, he would give the lakefront part of the camp that is cleared between the tabernacle and the lake.

When he told them that he would give the lake front, they wanted to go right then to see Mr. Bowman. Mr. Bowman said that he would sell it

This is the original drink stand that was later moved farther down the cove and incorporated into the longer fishing pier.

to them for two thousand dollars. Arthur gave him one hundred dollars to bind the trade. The Rev. Willard Preslar and Arthur each gave a thousand a piece to hold it till the conference met the last of August. Before the week [was over], they [men from the conference] had

This photograph shows the entrance to the youth camp that Arthur and Isma supported with their financial donations and their significant donations of time and labor.

lumber on the ground and were building the kitchen. They used it for the tabernacle, and they slept in tents. They built a furnace, and the ones that spent the night cooked their breakfast on the furnace. The different churches around Lenoir and our church brought dinner. The first night they had services by lantern light. They were working on the power line, but didn't have it done in time for the first service.

I will go back to the thirties and tell you about the girls [since] I have been telling you about the boys. First, I will tell you about Millie when she was little. She always loved cats and dogs. It seemed that all the stray dogs and cats that people didn't want they would turn loose at the bridge. They [the animals] would come up to the house, and Millie would beg to keep them. One time we had 14 cats. She would sit in her little rocking chair and rock her kittens. One day she said she had prayed for a white cat. So when the mama cat had kittens, one of them was white. She was the happiest little girl in the world. She loved her cats, but I think she loved Mary Mae better than anything or anybody. She would watch for the car when Mary Mae came home from work, and she would say, "Have you got me anything?" She most always had something for her. She appreciated anything she brought. She would throw her little arms around Mary Mae's neck and say, "When I get big and you get little, I will get something for you."

When she [Millie] was ten years old, she would catch the city bus to go to her music lessons twice a week. We had a big German Shepherd dog. Lady would go with her up to the highway, [and] sit beside her till the bus came. When Millie got on, then Lady would come home.

In August 1947, Mary Mae came home from Charlotte on her vacation and said she was going to take me and Dad on our honeymoon -- just a weekend trip to the mountains. We left early Friday morning. Mary Mae said, "Dad likes to see pretty crops growing, so we will drive by Shelby, then to Lake Lure, Chimney Rock and through Linville Caverns to Asheville, Canton, Waynesville then across to Sylva, Bryson City and Cherokee." We spent that night at a motel, the last one before you get to the mountains at Newfound Gap. I will always remember that breakfast. The dining room was a screened porch on the banks of a small stream. You could see the water and hear it gurgling as it passed over the rocky bottom of the creek. We had country cured mountain ham with eggs, homemade hot biscuits with grits and red eye gravy. It was terribly foggy

Saturday morning. We were afraid to start up over the mountain to Gatlinburg. It was still so foggy when we got to the top of the mountain.

Isma, Arthur, and Millie Kate on the 1947 "honeymoon" trip.

We went out to Clingman's Dome, thinking maybe it would clear and the fog would lift, but it didn't. We came back down the mountain. We stopped at Lake Junaluska at the Methodist Campground. We ate dinner in Asheville and just took our time coming down the mountain, stopping at a lot of places to look at the scenery. We got home about seven o'clock tired, but happy with enough pleasant memories to last a lifetime. [We returned] home from our honeymoon after 35 years [of marriage] with our two dear daughters Mary Mae, 32, and Millie, 13. I have pictures taken on that trip that bring back happy memories – one of Mary sitting high on a rock at Clingman's Dome and one of Millie sitting beside a pond where the water was pouring in at a fish hatchery where we stopped way back in the mountains.

The week before Christmas, 1947, we had gone to town. When we came home, Cliff had his well-rig set up and was driving us a well. That was the nicest Christmas present we ever received.

The next week he drilled a well for Forest, and the first of the year, he drilled Allen's well. It was a busy summer in Huffman's Cove, 1948. Forest and Allen were building their homes , and they [the Advent Christian Conference] were building the tabernacle and girls dorm at the Camp.

They weatherboarded the old tabernacle halfway up the wall and screened in the other half, made tables and benches, and used it for a kitchen. It had two wood stoves with a hot water tank hooked to each one, two ice boxes, and a large double sink for dishes. The different churches in the conference gave dishes, silver, pots and pans, and each church sent a box of groceries and fresh vegetables. They asked me to be head cook. Two ladies from the First Church in Lenoir helped me with the meals. Their names were Mammie Holloway and Bessie Raby. Three or four women would come in every day to help with the dishes. That way I got acquainted with most all of the leading ladies of the different churches and made friendships that have lasted through the years. Some of the most pleasant memories I have are working with different ladies of the conference. That is why it means so much to me to go to conference gatherings. I learned a lot about running a camp the first summer. When I planted my garden, I planted for camp just like I did for my own freezer.

Cliff Huffman (left) with his first well drilling rig, circa 1947.

For salads for camp, I always planted cabbage, onions, carrots, cucumbers, and tomatoes.

When I killed my old hens in the Spring, I dressed about a dozen and put them in the freezer for camp. That way they were always ready. I could dress them before camp, and all I charged for them is what I could have gotten in the market not dressed.

I could not take care of our milk and leave home at five o'clock in the morning, so Dad milked and strained the milk in gallon jars, and we sold it to the camp for 40¢ a gallon. We had a big Guernsey cow that gave five gallons a day. It was plenty for camp.

I looked after and tried to save for camp like I did my own home. I spent two weeks out of the year for 11 years from '48 to '59 cooking at camp. Looking back at those years, they were the happiest weeks of my life. Not because I was receiving money for my work, but [because] I have been paid over and over with spiritual blessings. [I have] peace of mind knowing I have been a little help to young people of the conference. By not charging for my work and saving on food, we could make the fee cheaper so more young people could come, and I feel I had a part in making their stay pleasant because all young people love to eat.

I think of all the young people that have gone into full-time Christian service that used to come to camp. Some of our finest ministers in the Piedmont Conference are these men. They are Hal Vannoy, Floyd Boston, Leonard Boston, Banks Setzer, Kenneth Pritchard, and Roger Byrd. Those that have gone to the mission field are Margaret Helms, Marvin Casey, [and] Pat Helms in the Mission office.

Virginia Spencer and Millie Huffman married ministers and are working alongside their minister husbands. Shirlee Sherril married a minister also. In '48 we had the Christianaires Quartet, ministerial students from our [Advent Christian] school in Boston, now Berkshire Christian College. They made fine counselors. Their names were Floyd Powers, now head of our mission work in Japan; Oral Collins, now teaching at Berkshire Christian College; Dave Osborne, a successful pastor in the New England States; and Everet Ranson, now the pastor in Napa, California. It is interesting to read the church papers and see what progress different young people have made in the last twenty years.

Then I have met so many leaders from our schools that came to speak at our camp. From Aurora College, [there was] Dean Perry, Jerry Richardson, Travis Carter, and Pomeroy Carter. From Berkshire College, [there were] Ariel Ainsworth, Carlyle Roberts, Clinton Taber, and Allen Hodges. Knowing all these fine people gives you spiritual strength. I never would have met half the people I have as friends today if I had not been cooking at camp. Here is where I get my joy, and it is something money can't buy.

The spring of 1953, Millie graduated from High School. She got a job in a law office typing for Bill Chambee and a Mr. Reed. A group of students from New England School of Theology came through visiting churches, and two young men spent the night at our house. They were Bob Shepard and Roland Griswold. They begged her to come to school up there that fall. She told them she would work a year [and] then she would come.

One night about the middle of August, Millie and I had gone to prayer meeting. For some reason, Grandma didn't go. Dad didn't go in the summer months. He always stayed at the fishing pier till most people had gone home.

Millie and I were alone coming home. She hadn't said anything till we were halfway home. She said, "I am between the devil and the deep sea." I said, "Just jump in the sea, [but] don't let the devil get you," and laughed. She said, "Well, it is not funny." Then she told me what it was all about. She wanted to go to our Christian College. I told her we didn't have the money to send her, and she said, "I would scrub floors to go." I began to make her a new wardrobe. She would need warmer clothes up there. Her brothers gave her $50 a piece to pay her tuition. The first semester, she cleaned house and babysat. The first of the year, she got a job in a print shop after school and on Saturday.

The summer of '53, I realized that when Millie went off to school, I wouldn't have a chauffeur. If I wanted to go places, I would have to learn to drive. Arthur was at the fishing pier all the time, so I learned to drive. Millie taught me before she went away. I was 58 when I learned to drive.

Arthur's brother, Uncle Bob, said when I told him I had learned to drive, "You need to have a little wreck to make a good driver to make sure you realize how quick it can happen."

In a few weeks, I had just that. I was driving out from over at the pier. When I got to the top of the hill and started around the bend in the road, I realized the gas pedal was stuck. I was going faster than I was used to driving, so I turned off the switch and put on the brakes, but I was already a foot over the bank of the road. The ground was wet. The car just trembled a little, slid off the bank, and turned up on two wheels. If [the car] would have turned over, it would have been in the lake. Arthur and some gentlemen saw the car turn up on two wheels. They came and got me out. I didn't have a scratch, but I was scared. I didn't realize how bad till that night after I went to bed.

The only thing Arthur said to me about the wreck when he came and saw me in the car was, "Are you hurt?"

"No," I replied.

"Why did you do it?" Arthur asked.

Christmas 1953 on Huffman's Cove. Left to right, front row: Barbara, Granny Mary, Mary Mae, Steve, Isma, Arthur, Jerry, Suzanne, Danny, Janice, and Allen, Jr. Back Row: Millie Kate, Louise, McCoy, Rachel, Kay, Hal, Cliff, Jennie, Horace, Jeanette, Forest, Evelyn, Allen, Hanley Painter, and Lorene Huffman Painter.

All seven children gathered for Christmas 1954. Seated l to r: Mary Mae, Isma, Arthur, Millie. Standing l to r: Cliff, Allen, McCoy, Forest, and Hal.

"The gas pedal stuck," I said. They helped me out of the car. I came home and called a wrecker, got supper, did the chores, [and] went to bed about ten o'clock. I could not go to sleep. I called to Arthur and said, "Come sleep with me. It seems like the walls are closing in on me." He came, and I went to sleep. Next morning at breakfast after he said the blessing, his hand was laying on the corner of the table. I reached over and laid my hand over his and said, "Thank you, Dad, for not fussing at me about the car."

He said, "It is done. Let's forget it."

One morning in September 1953, Joe and Joanne Baucom, Margaret Helms, Virginia Spencer, and Millie with Joe's car piled high with luggage left for Boston. That was the lonesomest day I had spent in my married life. I could not bring myself to go upstairs to her room. I knew she was gone. It would never be the same.

Then I thought, the Lord has blessed us with seven fine children who were all out on their own doing well and had never given us any cause for headache. Then I realized how thankful I ought to be.

At Christmas time, two carloads of students came to North Carolina. Roland [Griswold] drove his car with Margaret, Virginia, Millie, and the President of the school, Carlyle Roberts.

Sometime the first of the year, we received a call from President Roberts asking if we were willing for our daughter, Millie, to become engaged to Roland Griswold. He had bought her a ring. They were not supposed to become engaged while in school. They told her she could wear it on a chain around her neck till school was out.

They came home Easter vacation. Linwood Loudon and Betty Kelly came along. Millie bought material for her wedding dress. They had set the date for June 19, 1954. They went back to school, and I went to making her wedding dress [and] also part of the bridesmaids' dresses and made mother a lavender dress for the wedding and a pink lace dress for myself.

At Christmas 1950, Millie gave me a diary. So I can give you a record of how I lived the first few months of 1951.

Jan. 1, 1951 – I took down and put away the Christmas decorations today. Tonight taught Distinctive Doctrine to Sunday School Council.

Millie Kate Huffman with her fiancée Roland Griswold, circa 1954.

Jan. 2, 1951 – Feeling fine, washed and ironed today. Cliff struck water at 225 feet drilling well for Allen. Weather partly cloudy and warm.

Jan. 3, 1951 – Went to town this morning, signed deed for Forest's land. Tonight went to semi-annual business meeting at church.

Jan. 4, 1951 – Worked in the house this morning; set out boxwood this afternoon. Cliff and Jennie, Hal and Rachel came for a while tonight.

Jan. 5, 1951 – Cleaned upstairs this morning, helped clean chicken house and fix lettuce rows. Clear and warm today.

Jan. 6, 1951 – Clear and warm, cleaned house this morning, cleaned the church this afternoon and fixed the communion for service tomorrow.

Jan. 7, 1951 – Cold today, taught Distinctive Doctrine to Mrs. Terry's class. Went to see Fleta and my brother Arthur this afternoon, to church tonight.

Jan. 8, 1951 – Cold today, washed this morning, read in my new book *Comprehensive Analysis of the Bible* this afternoon.

Jan. 9, 1951 – Cold today, helped butcher, made sausage, fried out lard, went to WHFM meeting tonight at Rev. Butterfield's.

Jan. 10, 1951 – Not quite so cold today, canned pork and sausage. Went to prayer meeting tonight [and] had good meeting.

Jan. 11, 1951 -- Partly cloudy and warm, ironed this morning. My knee giving me trouble this afternoon, not feeling well.

Jan. 12, 1951 – Weather still warm, haven't been well, in bed till noon, rheumatism in knee.

Jan. 13, 1951 – Feeling better today, cleaned kitchen this morning, helped Millie clean church this afternoon, raining.

Jan. 14, 1951 -- My birthday, went to church morning and night. All children home during the day except Mary. Cloudy with showers.

Jan. 15, 1951 – Cold and windy. I pieced a quilt top today. Cliff started Forest's well. Danny is spending his first night with us.

Jan. 16, 1951 – Clear and cold today. I made Danny a pair of pants this morning, cut quilt squares this afternoon, visited Cliff tonight.

Jan. 17, 1951 – Clear and warm, made Danny another pair of pants. Cloyd and Sarah Miller visited us this afternoon, ate dinner with us, enjoyed them a lot.

Jan. 18, 1951 -- Bright sunny day. I cooked dinner for Cliff and three of his men. He finished Forest's well and moved out.

Jan. 19, 1951 – Beautiful day, sowed lettuce this morning, washed this afternoon, Duke Power put a line to Allen's place and gave us more power.

Jan. 20, 1951 – Mary Mae home today. I ironed and cleaned house.

Jan. 21, 1951 – Went to church morning and night, had dinner with Jessie and Ben; all children ate supper with us except Cliff's and Coy's families.

Jan. 22, 1951 – Clear and cold today, finished a quilt top today, not feeling well, going to bed early.

Jan. 23, 1951 – Freezing rain today, made a quilt top for WHFM, Juanita Bowman spending the night with Millie.

Jan. 24, 1951 – Clear today, washed this morning, visited Artie this afternoon, this evening Dad helping Cliff.

Jan. 25, 1951 – Ironed this morning, mended this afternoon, Dad helping Cliff put in Forest's pump.

Jan. 26, 1951 – Cold, went to town this morning, cleaned the church this afternoon.

Jan. 27, 1951 – Cleaned house this morning, planted sugar peas this afternoon.

Jan. 28, 1951 – Went to church morning and evening, Rev. Faulkingham spoke in the morning and Rev. Roberts at night, went to see Aunt Julia today.

Jan. 29, 1951 – Partly cloudy and warm, haven't worked too hard today, just did house work and made hominy, Forest finished his road [drive to his new house on the opposite side of the lake].

Jan. 30, 1951 – Rainy and cold, did some mending, worked over a dress.

Jan. 31, 1951 – Misting rain, turning to ice, didn't get to prayer meeting, ice freezing on windshield.

Feb. 1, 1951 – Cold and windy, washed forenoon, pieced two quilt tops this afternoon.

Feb. 2, 1951 – Cold down to 13° above this morning, ironed and mended today, Juanita and Betty spending the night with Millie.

Feb. 3, 1951 – Cold, haven't felt well, worked in kitchen this morning, in bed part of afternoon, helped Jeanette with blouse.

Feb. 4, 1951 –Went to church morning and night, Cliff ate dinner with us, Jennie's birthday next week, still cold today.

Feb. 5, 1951 – Clear and cold today, sewed on dress for Mother.

Feb. 6, 1951 – Partly cloudy, washed in afternoon, mended this evening.

Feb. 7, 1951 – Windy and cold, put up quilt this morning, worked on mother's dress this afternoon.

Feb. 8, 1951 – Cold, ironed this morning, quilted this evening.

Feb. 9, 1951 – Snowed all day, I quilted all day.

Feb. 10, 1951 – Warmer today, prepared dinner to take to Uncle Bud and Aunt Lola's 56th Wedding Anniversary tomorrow.

Feb. 11, 1951 – Went to church morning and evening, went to Uncle Bud and Aunt Lola's wedding anniversary dinner.

Feb. 12, 1951 – Clear warm, quilted all day.

Feb. 13, 1951 – Still clear and warm, washed this morning, went to Artie's a little while this evening, then quilted till night, went to the WHFM Meeting.

Feb. 14, 1951 – Clear and warm, finished quilt this morning, put fertilizer to boxwood this evening, went to prayer meeting tonight.

Feb. 15, 1951 – Partly cloudy and warm, ironed and packed dishes to take to Parish Hall for Father-Son Banquet, Saturday night.

Feb. 16, 1951 – Rainy, stayed with Kay while Rachel went to Dentist, went to town to get groceries for banquet, dressed chickens for banquet.

Feb. 17, 1951 – Cooked chickens for banquet this morning, helped fix banquet this evening, clear and warm.

Feb. 18, 1951 – Went to church morning and night. Forest's and Coy's families ate dinner with us; all children here during the day.

Feb. 19, 1951 – Still warm, got out fertilizer for Dad to drill on pasture.

Feb. 20, 1951 – Helped put fertilizer on alfalfa today.

Feb. 21, 1951 – Washed today, went to prayer meeting tonight, clear.

Feb. 22, 1951 – Got out fertilizer for Dad to sow oats today, windy.

Feb. 23, 1951 – Ironed today and made hot bed for starting plants.

Feb. 24, 1951 – Cleaned house this morning, planted potatoes, set out cabbage plants this evening, made cake, dressed chickens, churned.

Feb. 27, 1951 – Washed and set out boxwood, clear and warm.

Feb. 28, 1951 – Ironed today, went to prayer meeting tonight.

Feb. 29, 1951 – Helped sow lespedeza today, still warm.

March 1, 1951 – Went to town, shoes for Millie, also dress and shoes for myself.

March 3, 1951 – Cleaned house this morning, helped Forest and Net sow grass on road bank.

March 4, 1951 – Went to church morning and night, ate dinner with Hal and Rachel, a steak dinner, yum-yum!

March 5, 1951 – Helped bale hay today, went to board meeting at church tonight.

March 6, 1951 – Made myself an organdy blouse, hemmed a skirt, Artie, Vervie, and Keith's wife visited me this afternoon.

March 7, 1951 – Washed this morning, finished Mother's dress this morning, went to prayer meeting tonight.

March 8, 1951 – Ironed this morning, sowed lespedeza seed this afternoon, and raked flower garden.

March 9, 1951 – Washed curtains this morning. Helped Dad make pump house this afternoon. Ossie Preslar and Ned's wife came this evening.

March 10, 1951 – Worked in the kitchen this morning, ironed curtains, and put them up this afternoon, am tired, but feel good.

March 11, 1951 -- Went to church morning and night, Rev. Butterfield had good sermons, enjoyed them a lot.

March 12, 1951 – Made myself a dress today, cloudy and cold.

March 13, 1951 – Fixed refreshments for WHFM meeting tonight, still cloudy and warm.

March 14, 1951 – Washed today, still cold, not well today.

March 15, 1951 – In bed most of the day, flu.

March 16, 1951 – Ironed today, could hardly stay up.

March 17, 1951 – In bed most of day, still feeling tough.

March 18, 1951 – Not able to go to church, missed going a lot.

March 19, 1951 – Feeling a little better, finished my dress today.

March 20, 1951 – Washed this morning, went to church tonight.

March 21, 1951 – Ironed this morning, went to church tonight.

March 22, 1951 – Fixed communion bread for service tonight, had a wonderful service, best we have ever had.

March 23, 1951 – Cleaned house this morning and worked in garden, helped clean church this afternoon.

March 24, 1951 – Got ready for Easter tomorrow, made corsages, made cake and salad, dressed chicken, Mary came home today.

March 25, 1951 – Went to sunrise service, also morning and evening services, enjoyed them all, all children home during the day.

March 26, 1951 – Helped Net make her first garden, windy.

March 27, 1951 – Washed this morning, cleaned boxwood this evening.

March 28, 1951 – Set out boxwood and ironed today, went to prayer meeting, had good service.

March 29, 1951 – Made cookies and cleaned house, also dressed chickens for tomorrow night supper.

March 30, 1951 – Mr. and Mrs. Ackerman, Rev. and Mrs. Butterfield and Jim ate with us, enjoyed them a lot, good fellowship.

March 31, 1951 – Cleaned brooder house in forenoon, helped sow grass in backyard in afternoon, clear and windy.

April 1, 1951 – Went to church morning and night, visited Aunt Emma this afternoon, took her violets and cookies, clear and warm.

April 8, 1951 – Went to church morning and evening, have a new Ford.

April 9, 1951 – Gathered first lettuce today.

April 10, 1951 – Went to town in forenoon, cleaned boxwood this evening.

April 11, 1951 – Washed this morning, called Burwells's to bring me a new Easy Washer.

April 12, 1951 – Gathered lettuce today, let me explain what I mean by gathering lettuce. We had about a quarter of an acre sowed in Grand Rapids leaf lettuce. We would pull it up by the roots, place it in bushel baskets with tops to the outside of the basket and roots in the middle of the basket. When I say I gathered lettuce, I mean 5 or 6 bushels.

April 13, 1951 – Ironed today.

April 14, 1951 – Cleaned house and prepared dinner for tomorrow.

April 15, 1951 – Went to church morning and night, Rev. Butterfield's and the Terry's ate dinner with us.

April 16, 1951 – Washed today, planted beans and gathered lettuce.

April 17, 1951 – Ironed, fertilized boxwood, replanted beans, cleaned flower gardens.

April 18, 1951 – Gathered lettuce today, helped put up quilt at Parish Hall tonight for WHFM Society.

April 19, 1951 – Stayed at boat house while Dad went to town, cleaned upstairs this evening.

April 20, 1951 – Cleaned kitchen this morning, helped quilt at Parish Hall this evening.

April 21, 1951 – Went to church morning and night, started to make out grocery list to send to churches of the conference for food for Camp.

This is the last of my diary. With gardening, canning, and freezing to do, I just forgot half the time to write when night came around.

Now I will finish telling you about Millie's wedding. School was out June the second, and they were getting married June 19, so Roland brought Margaret Helms, Virginia Spencer, and Millie home. He was going to pastor the Charlotte Church starting the 10th. The wedding was in the Hickory Advent Christian Church. Arthur gave the bride away, [and] Mary Mae was Maid of Honor. Bridesmaids were Virginia Spencer, Lorene [Huffman Painter], Net [Huffman] and one of Roland's cousins. Janice [Huffman] was the flower girl. Ushers were Hal, Forest, Horace,

[and] McCoy. Guy Ingle was Best Man. They were married at four o'clock June 19, 1954.

They stayed with us that summer. I had arthritis in my knee, and Millie helped with canning and freezing vegetables. They would go to

Arthur Huffman and Millie Kate are pictured on her wedding day, June 19, 1954. Isma made the wedding dress on her Singer sewing machine.

Charlotte a couple days a week to visit church members. The first of September, they went back to Boston to go to school. Millie didn't go to school. She kept house and worked in a print shop to help Roland finish the year. Now after 15 years and [with] her two girls in school, Millie finally finished college.

Now we are back where we started. The children were all gone. Arthur and Mother and I were all alone. Mother was 85, and her mind was getting poor. She stayed in her room most of the time looking through her closets and dresser drawers. She saved every piece of material, string, or button she could find and put them in her dresser drawer.

Mother had always been well, and for the last fifteen years, she didn't have a care in the world. She lived with us, and she had bought the old home place, and she had rooted and set out boxwood. That was all the responsibility she had, and it was something she liked to do. She worked hard with the boxwood, but she enjoyed it and kept them in good shape. When you are doing what you like to do, it isn't work. It is just good exercise. I think that is the reason Mother lived to be eighty-eight.

In June 1955, Roland graduated and took a church in Orlando, Florida. They came by and stayed with us a few days on their way to Florida.

One evening in July, Arthur came home from the fishing pier all excited. He said he wanted to go with Cliff hunting in Wyoming that fall. He said if I could tend the pier while they were gone, I could go with Mary Mae to see Millie when they got back. I said fine. They left August 29 and got back the last of September.

On the second Saturday in October at 6 o'clock in the morning, Mrs. Basil Spencer, Mary Mae, and I left for Florida. We spent Saturday and Sunday night with our former pastor and wife, Rev. and Mrs. Butterfield at Jacksonville. We really had a nice time. Monday we went to Orlando and spent two weeks with Roland and Millie. Mrs. Spencer went to Melbourne to visit Harold and Virginia. Roland took us to Cypress Gardens, Melbourne Beach, West Palm Beach, Miami Beach, [and] then across the state to St. Petersburg and Tampa. He took us all over Orlando. There are so many lakes in Orlando. It is a beautiful town.

In June 1957, I read a letter from Millie asking if I would consider being head cook at Dowling Park Camp Meeting [held] the middle of August for ten days. She said I could bring my own help from North Carolina.

My sister and brothers said Mother could visit them while I was away, so I decided to go. I got ladies that helped at camp here in July. They were Lillian and Nadine Duncan and Mrs. Dan Whisnant from Lenoir.

They always have Youth Camp at Dowling Park the week before Camp Meeting, so Roland and Millie had brought a group of young people from their church up to camp. On Wednesday, Roland came up to Charlotte to meet with the Board of the Charlotte Church, and I went back with him. Camp Meeting started the next Tuesday. By being there ahead of time, I could see the kitchen in operation by the staff that was there for Youth Camp. I had to go to Lake City to the wholesale house and order food for a ten-day Camp Meeting. Not knowing how many would be there, they told me to order everything wholesale. We took inventory of what was in the kitchen before camp started and what was in it when we left. They said we had fed the people for a little less than a dollar a day.

On Saturday evening after I had stopped at Lake City and put an order for groceries to be delivered on Monday, we left for Orlando. Roland had a big station wagon. Millie, Roland, and I were in the front seat, 4 girls in the back seat, and 2 boys laying up behind the seat and their luggage strapped on top of the station wagon. We were off to Orlando. We spent the weekend in Roland and Millie's home.

Monday evening, we headed back to Dowling Park. When we got to camp, Lillian, Nadine, Mrs. Whisnant, and the man with the groceries were waiting for us. We got the groceries put away and luggage put away. We were ready to start cooking Tuesday morning.

The weather was awfully hot. We had three electric fans in the kitchen, and we got along OK. We worked hard, but we met a lot of good Christian people that I never would have met had I not gone down there to cook that summer, and bonds grew closer to the ones that went along and helped cook. It was the first trip to Florida for each of us. Lillian drove her car back home. The trip was filled with good fellowship. These are precious memories that will linger as long as I live.

The spring of '58, Arthur sold our last horse and bought a rototiller and a new 20 foot freezer so I could tend a big garden and have plenty of room to freeze the vegetables. I enjoyed working and keeping a good clean garden. I used the tiller to keep my boxwood clean.

Arthur stayed at the fishing pier from 5:30 a.m. till 10:00 at night, so he had no time to work around the house or in the garden.

Mother's mind was getting worse all the time. She would go over to the old place and look at her boxwood and come back. One morning the middle of September, she got up [and] put on her clothes, but she didn't speak. She didn't talk much any time, but when I spoke to her and she didn't answer, I knew there was something wrong. I called the doctor, and he said she had a blood clot. He said she would be as well off at home as in the hospital. If I could keep her comfortable, she would be better satisfied. Artie was over at Keith's when Skipper was born, and Carl was in the hospital with ulcers, and Arthur [Moretz] was home sick.

The first week I took care of her myself, and the doctor came every day. After the first week, Artie came and stayed as long as mother lived. She passed away October 23 at 5:00 p.m. The funeral was at the First Advent Christian Church of Hickory, NC, at 2 o'clock in the afternoon

Mary Louise Teague Moretz Huffman poses for a portrait with her second husband, Dr. Daniel Monroe Huffman.

Mary Teague Moretz Huffman's grown children meet, circa 1955. Left to right: Arthur Moretz, Isma Moretz Huffman, Mary Teague Moretz Huffman, Carl Moretz, and Artie Moretz Starnes.

October 25, 1958. Services were conducted by Rev. M. G. Butterfield and Rev. Cecil Noble. The choir sang "The Lord is My Shepherd," and Rev. Hal Vannoy sang "My Jesus as Thou Wilt." Burial was in Catawba Memorial Park.

It sure was lonesome around here that fall. I was all alone till it got too cold for Arthur to stay at the fishing pier.

I did a lot of sewing that winter. When spring came, I tended my boxwood. I planted a large garden so we would have plenty to can and freeze and have a lot of corn, beans, potatoes, tomatoes, cabbage, onions, cucumbers, [and] squash to use at camp. I had the nicest garden that year. It was 1958. Arthur had gone to the stock sale, our grandson Danny was staying at the pier, and I was working in the garden and enjoying every minute of it. I always felt in partnership with the Lord and closer to Him when I was working in the garden than anything else I did.

That day I took up three bushels of onions, dug eight bushels of Irish potatoes, and pulled up the old sugar pea vines. [I was] getting ready to plant late roasting ear corn. Arthur came home from the stock sale, and Danny came to the house and helped me plant the corn. The next day I went over everything that was planted in the garden with the tiller. There hadn't been a weed anywhere. It had been a good season, and the garden was beautiful. That was the last time I used the tiller.

On Monday morning July 1, 1959, when I got up Arthur said, "I don't want an egg this morning. I just want a cup of coffee and a bowl of cereal." I put the coffee on to perk, fixed him a bowl of Cornflakes, and cut up a banana on them. That was the last thing I did with my right hand.

Christmas 1972 – Seated: Millie, Arthur, Isma, Mary Mae; Standing: Cliff, Jennie, Allen, Evelyn, McCoy, Louise, Forest, Jeanette, Hal, and Rachel.

Christmas 1984 – Front Row: Mary Mae, Jeanette, Forest, Cliff; Back Row: Allen, Millie, Evelyn, Louise, McCoy, Jennie, Rachel, and Hal.

I came to the den and picked up my apron off a chair and tried to put it on, but my right arm was just hanging there limp at my side. I walked into thc bedroom, sat down on the edge of the bed, and called for Arthur. [I] told him my arm was paralyzed. It felt like there were cogs grinding together in the left side of my head, and I was sick to my stomach. He said I had better lie down. He helped me to get laid back on the bed and went to call the doctor and kids. I don't know too much that happened the next couple weeks. They [The doctors] kept me in Richard Baker Hospital ten days, [and] then took me to Charlotte Memorial for four or five weeks. They x-rayed my head and neck, tapped my spine, [and] wrapped my leg with an elastic bandage from the end of my toes to my body. They would rewrap it every morning. I wore that for six weeks after I came home, and [I] took therapy for three years twice a day till Arthur had a heart attack, and he wasn't able to give me therapy any more. I can't use my hand, but I am so thankful to God that I can walk and am able to do work with Arthur's help. He ties my shoes and apron, does the mopping and sweeping, and helps with the dishes. I do the cooking, make the beds, [and do] the dusting, vacuuming, and tidying up the house. I tend the washing, and he hangs out and brings in the clothes, and I do the ironing. I do most of my sewing, and I just love to get out while it is cool in the morning and the birds are singing and hoe in the garden. I have to use one hand, but I love to do it anyway. I hope I can have a garden as long as I live.

Up to 1959 [when] I had a stroke, we had always had a family get together either at Thanksgiving or Christmas here at the home, but since the family had gotten so large, we didn't have room. Forest and Hal each

Isma and Arthur Huffman celebrated their 50th wedding anniversary in 1963. The event was held at their home on Huffman's Cove. I remember Grandma saying that she prayed for nice weather. It was a beautiful day!

have a full basement in their homes, so we have been meeting with them. There are 41 in the family now in 1969. Children – 7; Grandchildren -- 17; Great-Grandchildren – 11.

On February 9, 1963, we were married 50 years. The children gave us a big celebration on Sunday, February 17, 1963. It wasn't on our anniversary, but it was the only time all the children could be there. It was the happiest day of my life. When I said that, a lot of people said, "You mean you are happier than you were on your wedding day 50 years ago?" and I said, "Yes. I have so much more to be happy for. I have a dear good husband, seven fine children that never give us any cause for heartache, and I can say the seventeen grandchildren and the eleven great-grandchildren are just something to love. We have a comfortable home and our church close by with hundreds of friends and neighbors that have visited us. Today anyone who wouldn't be happy with that set-up doesn't deserve to have happiness."

The last Sunday in August 1963 was Roland's last Sunday to preach at the Charlotte Church. They were all loaded and ready to leave right after services. Hal, Rachel, [and] the children took Dad and me. We packed a good picnic lunch. Mary Mae came over too. We all went over to the park below the church and had a good picnic before they left. They were going to pastor the Plainville, Connecticut church.

The last of October, Mary Mae came up from Charlotte on Friday evening, and we were all packed and ready to leave on Saturday to go visit Millie and family. We left at 4 o'clock in the morning. Mary said we were going to take our time and see all we could. We didn't go the nearest way, but the way she thought would be the prettiest that time of year. We went over to Wilkesboro and got on the parkway to Roanoke. Then we went up the Shenandoah Valley. We went all the way across West Virginia. We stayed at a new motel just across the Pennsylvania line. We spent all day Sunday crossing the whole length of the state of Pennsylvania. We took our time. I will always remember Pennsylvania more than any state we went through. We spent the night just this side of the George Washington Bridge at the Hudson River. Monday morning, Mary said she wanted us to see Bear Mountain Bridge. She had seen it when she went to Canada. We drove about 40 miles up the Hudson River and crossed the bridge. I am glad we went to see it, but I don't want to cross it again. We went from one little town to another for a couple of hours. We got to Millie's about one o'clock. Joyce and Melodie were playing in the yard. When they saw Mary's car, they ran all the way to the crossing to meet us.

Wednesday Roland took us to see Plainville Campground; [then on] Thursday [we went] up to Berkshire Christian College at Lenox, Massachusetts. We had dinner at the college, looked the grounds and buildings over, and visited with the professors and students we knew; then [we] came back by East Brookfield and had supper with Roland's parents. [We] got home about 12:00 p.m. [We] slept late on Friday morning, rested and got ready to leave [for North Carolina] early Saturday morning. [We] left about six o'clock, [and] we crossed the George Washington Bridge about sun up. [Then we] got on the New Jersey Turnpike. We stayed at a motel the other side of Richmond. We got home about 5 o'clock -- tired, but with a lot of pleasant memories.

Isma Moretz Huffman sits in the orchard, circa 1938.

I want to give you a little philosophy that will help you to come to the end of the way with love for humanity and a peace in your heart. I will give it in groups of three. The three dearest things to my heart are my family, my home, and my church; three kinds of work I love best [are] gardening, cooking (especially making yeast bread), and serving. [For] recreation, [I enjoy] visiting friends [and] reading good books, something educational and uplifting. Authors I like are Catherine Marshall, Faith Baldwin and Gladys Tabor. I love to walk through the woods in the spring. I will give you some verses I wrote on an imaginary trip to my sister Artie's house. Here it is:

As I walked a woodland path
One sunny day in Spring,
I saw the violets peeping through
A bed of dusty green.

The dogwood trees were bursting forth
A mass of snowy white,
A robin feeding by the path
While on its northward flight.

The stately poplars by the brook
Were all a misty green
And through the trees not yet in bud
The willows can be seen.

And coming nearer to the brook
I hear a gurgling sound
As water against the pebbles dash
While passing over the ground.

The alders on its mossy banks
With tags all bending down
An early bee is buzzing
Where the pollen can be found.

Amid such beauty this all
I fall upon my knees
And thank the Creator of it all
That I have eyes to see.

Take these words with you sometime and walk the wooded path to Aunt Artie's. When you come to those large spreading dogwood trees just before you cross the little brook, I guarantee you will feel like falling to your knees and [thanking] God for this great, big, wonderful, beautiful world.

The greatest blessings you get from life are free. They don't cost you a penny. Just use the senses God has given you – Feeling, Hearing, Seeing, Tasting, Smelling.

Things I love to feel – the soft breeze flowing through my hair on a warm spring evening [and] to sit barefoot on the bank of a small stream and feel the cool water running between my toes. [I love] the ecstasy I feel from a kiss from my husband and my children [and] the feel of the cold nose of my faithful collie dog welcoming me home.

Things I love to see – a beautiful sunset. There is one I shall never forget [because] it was so beautiful and unusual. There had come a thunderstorm and cleared up, [and] the sun was about an hour high. It was calm after the storm, [and] there wasn't a leaf stirring in the trees and the lake looked like a mirror. The hills on the other side of the lake were in wheat. It had been cut, and the field was full of wheat shocks. You could see all that reflected in the lake -- the wheat shocks on the hill with the old field pines for a background with one large forest pine standing like a sentinel over all. I have lived here 54 years, and that was the most beautiful sunset I have ever seen. I love to see starry nights, towering mountains, children playing, and waterfalls.

Things I love to hear – The first call of the birds in the Spring. The first I hear around our home says, "Jay bird, jay," and the mockingbirds are chattering all the time. Sometimes they holler at night. I love to hear the plaintive call of the whip-or-will. In the early spring, I love to hear frogs holler in the marsh at the head of the lake, and I loved the children's voices calling "Mom" when they came home from school.

Things I enjoy tasting – What could taste better than a drink of cold water fresh from a spring on the north side of a hill? I enjoy tasting wild strawberries, huckleberries, and chinkpins [chinquapins] that used to grow in fence corners of an old rail fence.

Things I love to smell – fresh turned sod after a shower of rain, mother's hedge of lilacs in bloom, a field of newly mowed hay just beginning to dry, [and] to wander through the woods and find a clump of trailing arbutus, the most sweet smelling wild flower I know.

Our home has always been open to good Christian people. The most pleasant memories I have are entertaining ministers and missionaries. Following are the names of the ones I have had in my home through the years.

Rev. Brown, Rev. Piercey, Rev. R. W. Cottrell, Rev. S. E. Gregg, Rev. N. W. Harrison, Rev. Victor Harrison, Rev. and Mrs. J. A. Downes, Rev. R. L. Isbell, Rev. C. R. Hankins, Rev. Lee Baker, Rev. Jerry Richardson, [and] Rev. Dean Perry. Missionaries [include] Dwight Banks, Rev. and Mrs. Fred Clothey, Berly Hollis, Mary Brown, Marion Damon, Floyd and Musa Powers, Margaret Helms, Rev. David Osborne, Charles Ransom, Rev. Everette Ransom, Rev. Garland Preslar, Rev. Floyd Boston, Rev. Leonard Boston, Rev. Hal Vannoy, Rev. Gordon Noble, Rev. Cecil Noble, Rev. S. E. Thrulow, Rev. Ronald Schoolcraft, Rev. M. G. Butterfield, Rev. Bill Mayo, Rev. Johnny Green, Rev. A. O. Turnbow, Rev. Banks Setzer, Rev. Alton Trivett, Rev. Fremont Whitman, Rev. Weldon Chambers, Rev. Will Ingle, Rev. Harrison Ingle, Rev. Tom Braswell, Rev. Roland Griswold, Rev. Bill Coughlin, Rev. H. L. Duncan, Re. Z. B. Duncan, Rev. Corbin Kiser, Rev. Charles Parker, Rev. Pomeroy Carter, Rev. Travis Carter, Rev. Ariel Ainsworth, Rev. Clinton Taber, Rev. Carlyle Roberts, Rev. Bob DuPriest, Rev. Fred Clothey, Jr., Rev. Don Wrigley, Rev. Fred Seafret, Rev. Louis Grandsee, Rev. Ronald Walton, Ina Hart, Rev. John Perry, Rev. Bob Shepard, Rev. Joe Johnson, Rev. Asa Johnson, Rev. Allen Hodges, Rev. Lorne Ross, Rev. Charles Foss, Rev. Chester Joyner, Rev. Frank and Susie Davis, Rev. A. E. Pender, Rev. Ray Bowden, Rev. and Mrs. Percy Grant,

Rev. C. L. Kirby, Rev. Raymond Beecraft, Rev. Harold Crocker, Rev. John Warren, Rev. H. A. Owens, Dr. J. Howard Shaw, Rev. Clarence DuBois, Rev. Vernon Burt, Rev. Leonard Lester, Rev. Earnest Tidball, Rev. Julius Parker, Rev. Jimmy Jenson, Rev. Joe Baucom, [and] Rev. William Bailey.

Some of these ministers who have been our pastors through the years we have entertained dozens of times. They have been a blessing to us; the older ones seem like fathers to us, [and] the younger ones like our sons.

By our entertaining so many Christian people, our children had a chance to meet a lot of good Christian people. I think they influenced their lives for good. The children are so good to us. I am proud of all 52 of them, that is children, grandchildren, and great-grandchildren. All are law-abiding citizens. Not one has ever been arrested. I have thanked the Lord so many times that there haven't been any vacant chairs left in the family. We sure have been blessed. I hope there won't be any while I live. I just passed the 75th milestone traveling toward the setting sun looking for a beautiful sunset.

On October 24, 1970, I am sitting here in the den looking across the lake at the beautiful foliage thinking of the past ten years since I had a stroke. I wonder if there is anything in my life these days that would be worth writing about that would be interesting to you children. Most of you live close by and know what happens in Huffman's Cove. You will never know how much it means to me when you drop by for a little chat.

Autumn is a time of mixed emotions for me; it's beautiful, happy, and sad. What could be more beautiful than walking on an old farm road on a warm October evening with the blue sky and a few fleecy white clouds overhead? On the road banks, clumps of goldenrod bloom. White, purple and blue asters mix with the dark red leaves of shoemake [sumac] and the scarlet of sassafras with here and there a small cedar. The hills in the background are ablaze with all colors and hues. It makes me stand in awe and thank God for the beauty of His creation.

I am always happy at Thanksgiving time when the crops are harvested and the frost is on the pumpkin and the corn is in the shock.

God has been good. He sends the sunshine and the rain. If we do our part, we have a bountiful harvest for which I am always thankful.

We have had the beautiful and happy time. Now we have to face the sad part. When I walk through the woods the last of November as the last of the leaves are floating down to the ground, I cannot help but think of Death. The rustling leaves, the frostbitten grass, [and] the barren trees all speak of Death. It is so sad till you think of the wisdom of God in creation. The leaves fall and decay and fertilize the trees while they are dormant. They rest for a while. In the Spring, they fill with the power of God in nature and are resurrected to a new life.

Once a year, all through our lives, we have a resurrection sermon, a sermon preached to us through nature if we will just stop, look, and listen.

Dying doesn't seem so sad to me as it used to. When that eternal day dawns, all that are in their graves shall hear the voice of Man and shall come forth -- they that have done good to the resurrection of life, and they that have done evil to the resurrection of damnation. When death overtakes us, it will be just like a dreamless sleep till the breaking of that eternal day when Gabriel blows his trumpet calling forth the sleeping dead.

You remember when Jesus was at Lazarus' grave he said, "He is not dead, but sleepeth." Death is sleep to the righteous. It will be a glad morning when all the redeemed of the Lord wake up in the resurrection morning. When death's prison bars are broken, we shall rise, Hallelujah, we shall rise!

I have written about each of you children as individuals. Now I want to write a few things about your Dad. You were too young to remember when these things happened, but are old enough now to appreciate them.

When we first bought this place, the first thing Dad did was terrace the land. After every hard rain before the grass dried off, you would see Dad with his shoes off, pants rolled to his knees, a shovel on his shoulder, looking the place over to see if the terrace had broken anywhere.

When I asked him why he was in such a hurry to repair the terraces, he said, "The few acres of God's good earth that I am responsible for I want to leave in as good a shape as I found it." That has been his motto for the 57 years we have lived here. He is almost 83 years old, but he still carries his shovel and bucket. He doesn't have to worry about the terraces because the whole place is seeded in fescue and has a good sod, but he goes after noxious weeds.

About seven or eight years ago, there came up in the pasture below the lower wall of the yard a patch of little yellow flowers about 10 feet square. The flower was shaped like a daisy and about half as big. There was just one stem from the ground with dozens of flowers in the top. They made beautiful arrangements. I used them a lot that summer. If I

Arthur and Isma are dressed for church, circa 1963.

had known they were such a pest, I could have pulled them up in 30 minutes. The till that carried the water from off the house went under the yard and emptied below the wall and above the patch of flowers. So the seeds were washed all over the hill. In two year's time, it was everywhere in the pasture. Dad mowed it down close. When it got dry, he burned it over. He carried his bucket, and if he saw a stray flower, he put it in the bucket, brought it to the house and let it get dry, and burned it. About three years of that kind of treatment, and we didn't see any more yellow daisies. I think your Dad has lived up to his motto to turn the land over to the next generation in a better shape than it was when he received it.

When you look out on the green hills of Huffman's Cove, remember that 150 years ago, it didn't look like that. While we went tending a crop, he had to keep up a continuous war to keep the soil from washing away. I know it is a great comfort to him now that he is not able to work to sit under the oaks and look at the green hills and know they are not washing away.

A lot of people have said to me, "I just love to drive out by Huffman's Cove and see the green hills and the lake." You see when you do something worthwhile in life, it is a comfort to you and a blessing to others.

I want to tell you a little more about myself. When you have passed 75 years, you realize you have crossed over the top and are going down the other side. It is not pleasant to speak of or think about, but it comes to each of us.

While thinking along that line a couple months ago, the thought came to me, "Why don't you take an inventory of the things you have in the house, such as pictures, vases, clocks, lamps, china, silver trays, plaques, luggage, [and] books. There are 44 children, grandchildren, great-grandchildren, and in-laws. I am putting the name of each individual on the article I want him to have. I think the gift will mean more to each child when they realize I wanted them to have it when Dad and I are gone.

Here are some more pleasant memories that have come to me while I have been sitting around not able to work like I used to. We didn't have a garden last summer, but the children, neighbors, and friends kept me in fresh vegetables all summer with plenty to freeze. I think how good people have been to us, and I wonder why till I remember what the Bible says in Ecclesiastes 11:1, "Cast thy bread upon the waters for thou shalt find it." Often many days I think one of the greatest pleasures I have had throughout the years was giving things away that I had raised in my garden.

Now after many days, I am receiving the bread I cast upon the waters. The Lord's promises are true and faithfully fulfilled through his children. The Bible says in Acts 20:35, "It is more blessed to give than to receive." I have gotten more real joy from giving something to someone who wanted that particular thing. I really do appreciate anything that is given to me, but real deep down joy comes from giving.

I told you at the beginning of this book that I thought I had been privileged to live in the 20th century. There has been so much change in every area of life.

Isma and Arthur Huffman with their collie dog, Ben, circa 1972.

I will tell you a few changes in my 76 years.

We will start with light – that and its source are the most important things to modern life. Around the turn of the century what everyone in the country used for lighting their homes was kerosene oil lamps or candles. In 1925, we bought a gas lamp. It was almost as good as an electric light. After the Rural Electrification Act of 1936 passed, power lines began to be strung all over the country. It began to be a different world. Now we could pump our water with electricity, cook our meals, refrigerate our foods, wash our clothes, heat our home, [and] run our TV, radio, toaster, mixer, vacuum, churn, clock, iron, [and we could] have an indoor toilet [and] run our freezer. Just what would we do without electricity!

I will tell you how I lived through the years. When I was small, we lived at home and boarded at the same place. Mother was a good manager and a good provider. We raised everything we ate. We raised our wheat for bread and some to sell. There was a corn mill. You see, all we had to do to have meal and flour was to go to the mill. They would take toll out of the wheat and corn for grinding, so you see we didn't need money.

We raised Irish and sweet potatoes, dry beans, dried apples and peaches, [and] dried corn. We would boil it [the corn] on the cob, then cut it off and spread it out to dry. You would have to soak it overnight when you wanted to cook it. We had a hardwood stand that would hold two bushels. We always made that stand full of kraut. We always put 3 or 4 layers of apples down in the kraut. The apples flavored the kraut. We raised our own hogs and cured hams, shoulders, and bacon. We kept a milk cow, [so we] always had milk and butter and cottage cheese. [We] raised our own chickens, [and we] always had a good garden in season.

In raising my own family, you can just repeat what you have already read, only make it larger. Instead of dried fruit, I canned it. There were nine of us in the family. I would can 300 half gallons of peaches, apples, [and] beans, 200 quarts [of] corn, soup mixture, pickles, jams, jellies, and bacon. [I] canned the boney meat and sausage. We always raised a beef cow every year and butchered and canned it. This is the part I played in helping take care of the physical needs of our family from 1913 till 1955. Then my work changed from canning to freezing. As our work gets less, our family gets less. We are back again to our family.

Now I will tell you about our recreation and entertainment socially and spiritually over a period of 70 years. From the time I was 8 years old, Mother would let me go and spend the night with my friends and cousins, and they would spend the night with me.

Once when I was spending the night at Uncle Tom's, he was going opossum hunting. My cousins all wanted to go along. They wanted me to go too. There were 4 of them – Bessie, Hattie, Joe, and Frank. They were used to going. Some of them always went with Uncle Tom. They were getting a big kick out of it. The boys would say "whoopee" to the dogs. I was afraid; the woods were dark and thick. All at once, they said he [the opossum] was treed. They all started walking fast. When we got over in the next hollow, there was old Rover with his front feet upon the tree as high as he could reach. Joe climbed up the tree and caught the possum by the tail. Tom cut down a little dogwood, split it, and drew the opossum's tail through the slit. Joe put the pole over his shoulder, and we went home. That was my first and last opossum hunt.

Mother always had our Grandpas and Grandmas, Aunts and Uncles, and cousins and friends to visit us. That is the way we entertained. Mother always took us to church and gathered us around that old long table in the kitchen and read the Bible to us. That was the way we got our spiritual food.

After we started a home of our own, there was hardly a weekend passed that we didn't have young couples our age or older for company. We have been friends through the years with most of them. Some of them have passed away. After the children grew up some, one of them usually had company.

A group of young people gathered around the piano singing hymns, folk songs, and carols at Christmas time was a joy to my heart and are pleasant memories today.

There were so many changes around the turn of the century. I was born at the right time to be in the middle of the change and see each side. The change in travel – Henry Ford's first automobile ran on the streets of Detroit, Michigan in 1896. I saw my first car in 1912 and took my first ride in 1914.

December 17, 1903, the Wright Brothers made their first flight. I saw my first airplane flight in Hickory October 1912.

Edison tested his first successful light bulb October 21, 1879. I don't remember when I saw my first electric light, but I sure remember when the power was brought to the country and we got our home lighted.

March 10, 1876, Alexander Graham Bell spoke the first words over a telephone. They were, "Mr. Watson, please come here. I want you." In 1914, the first telephone lines were put up out in the country. I spoke my first time on a phone in 1914.

The first idea of television was shown by Paul Nipkau, a German in 1880. [The idea was] then further developed in 1925 by C. Francis Jenkins of the USA and John L. Byrd of England.

In May 1894, Guglielmo Marconi, a young Italian sent radio signals ¾ of a mile on his father's estate. In 1899, he sent a message across the English Channel. Regular radio broadcasting began in the fall of 1920 when station WWJ in Detroit and KDKA in Pittsburg began their broadcast of the Harding-Cox election returns. That has been celebrated as the first great popular broadcasting event in history.

Refrigerators and freezers are another invention that have been a convenience to the home.

The washer and dryer and air conditioner are other conveniences.

All these wonderful inventions took place from 1879 to 1925.

Since then, they have done so many things [like] made computers, went to the moon, [and] put satellites in orbit. Yes, and we are using atomic power. The Atomic Energy Commission of the United States was appointed by the President in 1946 to develop knowledge of atomic energy and its uses.

The steam engine was the first machine that man created in order to produce power for himself. The first steam engine was developed in 1760 by James Watt. Just think. All these wonderful ways to travel were invented over a span of 50 years, most of them in my lifetime. What a wonderful time to be living!

When I was a child and heard people talk about the man in the moon, I never dreamed I would ever see a man walking on the moon.

THE END

And then . . .

What happened to this Catawba Valley family after Isma autographed copies of her *Memories Dedicated to My Grandchildren* as treasured Christmas gifts in December 1972?

Isma and her beloved husband Arthur lived in their home overlooking the waters of Huffman's Cove for two more years. With advancing age, they both became increasingly feeble and increasingly dependent on each other to make their independent life together still work. For sixty-one years, together they had faced crop failures, the Great Depression, sickness, and the uncertainty of sending sons off to war. Old age would be no different. Together they would face the end of their lives with faith in God and faith in each other.

On July 28, 1974, Arthur died of a sudden heart attack. He was 86 years old. Isma never fully recovered from her grief over Arthur's passing. She suffered a brain aneurism caused by a fall. She underwent brain surgery, but her health rapidly deteriorated, and she had to be placed in a nursing facility where she could receive the round-the-clock care she required. Just four months after Arthur's death, Isma joined him. She was 79 years old.

In February 1973, Arthur and Isma pose at their dining room table for a 60th Wedding Anniversary picture.

Isma and Arthur are together in their den, circa 1972.

A house full of children and grandchildren gathered for Christmas 1954. Seated on floor: Lorene Huffman Painter, Barbara, Suzanne, Danny, Allen Jr., Janice, Kay, Mary Mae, and Millie Kate. Seated on sofa: Forest, Jerry, Isma, Arthur, Granny Mary, Jennie, and Cliff. Standing: Hanley Painter, Rachel, Hal, Jeanette, Louise, Steve, McCoy, Evelyn, Allen, Peggy, and Horace.

Isma's seven children gather at a 1985 Huffman reunion. Front row: Cliff, Mary, Allen, and McCoy. Back Row: Millie, Hal, and Forest.

Jennie Lineberger Huffman and Horace Clifton Huffman celebrated their 50th Wedding Anniversary in 1982.

Five generations with Elijah Wilson Teague, Mary Teague Moretz Huffman, Isma Moretz Huffman, Cliff Huffman, and Lorene Huffman circa 1936.

Cliff Huffman chases a chicken with grandson Charles Painter, circa 1957.

Five Generations Proud! Seated: Mary Louise Teague Moretz Huffman, Isma Moretz Huffman, and Becky Huffman. Standing: Cliff Huffman, Horace Huffman, circa 1956.

The Cliff Huffman family gathers at the 1985 Huffman family reunion. Front: Jim Huffman, Belinda Huffman, Teresa Brown, Linda and Danny Huffman, David Huffman. Back: Hanley and Lorene Painter, Horace and Peggy Huffman, Jennie and Cliff Huffman, Jerry Huffman, and Janet Painter.

Mary Mae, Hal, and Millie enjoy a visit in 2002.

Mary Mae Huffman, pictured here in 1995, was always a welcome visitor from Charlotte to her many adoring nieces and nephews.

Mary Mae Huffman poses for a glamour shot sunbathing, circa 1955.

The Allen and Evelyn Huffman family attended a family gathering in 1985. Front row: Will, Mary Margaret. Middle Row: Allen, Jr., Trey Bradford, Barry, Evelyn, Allen, Sr. Back Row: Eddie Bradford, Janice Bradford, and Lisa Bradford.

Four cousins are part of Horace and Peggy Huffman's wedding party in 1954. Left to right: Suzanne, Kay, Steve, and Janice.

Allen, Allen, Jr., and Evelyn lived in St. Louis while Allen served in the Army. This picture dates 1944.

The McCoy Huffman Family in 1985. Front Row: Louise Huffman, McCoy Huffman holding his grandson Chris, Rhonda Huffman. Middle Row: Linda Barbour, Teresa Barbour Turpin, Barbara Huffman Barbour, and Phil Huffman. Back Row: Keith Barbour holding son Matt, Chip Turpin, Steve Huffman, Milford Barbour, and Jeffrey Barbour.

McCoy Huffman holds son Steve, circa 1953.

Forest and Jeanette take a boat ride on Huffman's Cove, circa 1949.

Forest, Hal and McCoy pictured in 2002.

Jeanette Baker was married to Forest Huffman at Mount Olive Lutheran Church on June 5, 1948.

Kay, Chip, Beth, and Mandy in 1962.

The Hal and Rachel Huffman family are pictured in September 2013. Seated: Rachel and Hal. Standing: Chip, Mandy, Beth, and Kay.

Rachel and Hal celebrate their 50th Wedding Anniversary in 1998.

Joy Griswold Gallagher was Isma's granddaughter who typed her 1967 and 1972 memoirs. Here Joy's family celebrates Christmas 2020.

Melodie Griswold competes with her horse Duke.

Millie Kate Huffman Griswold with her husband Dr. Roland Griswold .

In 1972, a Huffman Reunion was held at the Piedmont Youth Camp.

The Huffman siblings meet in 2002. Left to right: Millie, Jennie, Mary Mae, Evelyn and Allen, Forest and Jeanette, Louise and McCoy, Rachel and Hal.

Generation Three

Isma and Arthur left behind their seven adult children and many grandchildren and great-grandchildren, and today an ever-expanding family tree of descendants. They also left behind an enduring set of values that have been passed on from generation to generation.

Arthur's green hills are still reflected in the mirror of Lake Hickory. One of the huge oak trees still sinks it roots deep into the soil where Isma once hosted front yard family gatherings. Their legacy of hard work, their appreciation of nature's bounty, and their lives directed by a strong moral compass still resonate in the far-flung days of their descendants.

The next section of this book is entitled "Generation Three." It is a collection of memories from various children and grandchildren. Depending on birth order, the memories capture often quite different fragments of the complex web of family experience. Together, they present a more complete portrait of life on Huffman's Cove.

Growing Up on Huffman's Cove

Millie Kate Huffman Griswold

Seventh and Youngest Child of Arthur and Isma Huffman

I am the youngest child of the Arthur and Isma family. I was told that Mama said she wanted six children, and she'd "take any that came after that." I was number seven "the after that child." When I was born, Cliff, the eldest child, was already married and had daughter Lorene.

A nostalgic glance at the first eighteen years of my life on Huffman's Cove reminded me of principles taught me by my parents that have served me well during the past eighty-six years. Arthur and Isma gave me time, conversation, food, clothing, and a roof over my head. In addition, they modeled the Christian lifestyle. These things shaped my destiny.

When I was young, three generations lived under one roof, and we learned from each other. In 1940, Grandpa Daniel Huffman died shortly after they moved in with us, but Granny Mary lived with us for 18 years. Granny had no income. My parents supplied her daily needs; however, she did provide her own spending money by raising and selling lima beans and boxwood. I helped her shell lima beans to sell at the Fresh Air Market in Hickory, North Carolina. The beans were measured into a quart tin cup as they were shelled. The quart measure had to be "heaping full and running over" before she would pour it into the cloth sack. The market manager didn't re-measure the beans. He knew that if Granny said she had 15 quarts in the sack, it was true. Granny set an example of honesty.

Mary Louise Teague Moretz Huffman, circa 1953.

Truth and honesty were expected at our home. Once, while eavesdropping from the back porch, I heard my Dad refuse a job advancement because it required questionable dealings. I heard Dad choose integrity over financial gain. Another time, my brother Allen taught me honesty when I took a pencil from the church pew. He saw me writing with it and recognized the source of the pencil. In our home, only parents had pencils. Allen privately talked with me, and I agreed to return the pencil the next time we went to church. My parents never knew of the incident. As a teenager, if I skipped a worship service or justified my misbehavior by my friends' standards, Dad assured me that our family was different. We dared to be distinct; we dared to set our sails in a different direction; we dared to not be pressured into the world's mold. (By the way, I only skipped church once.)

My memory bank calls up reflections on friendship. Sunday dinner table was automatically set for eight people because the table would accommodate eight adults. If children were in the group, they ate at the kitchen table. After church, friends or family joined us for the meal. Church visitors and visiting ministers were often among these guests. The meal always included fried chicken, yeast rolls, homemade ice cream, and sweet tea. I learned table manners and the grace of hospitality through these gatherings. The guestroom was always ready. As I listened to the conversations of overnight guests, I determined to include some of their morals in my life.

From Mama, I learned to carry religious thoughts with me throughout the day. Each morning my sleep was interrupted with a cacophony of pots and pans rattling. I would hear Mama singing "Trust and Obey," as whiffs of bacon and eggs mounted the stairway to my bedroom. This music served as morning devotions by proxy from the overflow of a mother's heart.

My parents were committed to building a self-sustaining life through hard work and to serving Christ through His church. When the church doors opened, we were there. Mama and Granny were charter members of both the Fellowship Advent Christian Church in Alexander County and the First Advent Christian Church in Hickory. They held a variety of offices. Mama taught the Women's Sunday School Class for many years. Their lifestyle undoubtedly influenced my decision to accept Christ as my Savior and to enter full-time Christian service as a minister's wife and National Director of Christian Education for the Advent Christian Denomination.

When I "kicked the traces" and misbehaved, discipline was based on Ephesians 6:4 "bring them up in the discipline and instruction of the Lord." After an explanation by Dad or Mama as to why I deserved a switching, I was told "Now get a switch the size you deserve and bring it to me!" After the switching with stinging legs and teary eyes, I'd receive a gentle squeeze or hug that said, "You're forgiven. Go and don't do it again."

In a family that was heavily weighted towards boys, I was privileged to have the attention of a very kind, big-hearted sister, Mary Mae. She was like a second mother to me. Saturday night, we sat on the front porch steps and watched the full moon slide through the sky. Mary created an awe for the wonders of God's creation on these moonlit nights.

Millie Kate Huffman starts first grade in her new school clothes and new hairstyle provided by her beloved big sister, Mary Mae, circa 1940.

Often, we listened to the Grand Ole Opry from Nashville, Tennessee, on the radio. Mary's first employment was as a beautician. When I entered first grade, she gave me a perm, bought a blue dress, and took me to a professional photographer for my first photo. I was devastated when she moved to Charlotte to expand her job opportunities. I looked forward to her occasional weekend visits back home. She always brought me a treat, usually a pack of chewing gum.

Mary Mae Huffman at the Huffman Cove home place, circa 1950.

My penchant for piano was a prelude to Christian service. Mary bought the piano hoping to take lessons. It never happened, but I benefitted from her purchase. From my first piano lesson, I understood that learning piano was preparation for playing piano at First Advent Christian Church. Once a week after school, I rode the city bus to my piano lesson. My teacher lived near Lenoir-Rhyne College. The bus ride home brought me to within a mile or so of home. I walked the dirt road home from the bus stop. At some point, I was proficient enough to play a couple of hymns at Wednesday night prayer meeting. When Mrs. Ernest Whisnant bought a Hammond Organ for the church, I took a bus on Saturday to Charlotte for the six free lessons that came with the organ purchase. Then, I graduated to church organist. Each week I spent several hours practicing the organ. This training served me well in ministry. Often, I would be the instrumentalist in the churches Roland and I served. I offered beginning piano lessons in Plainville, Connecticut, to pay for my tuition at Connecticut State Teacher's College.

Growing up on Huffman's Cove involved a quiet environment, many chores, cats and a dog for playmates, swimming in the cove, learning by watching and listening to members of the family, and the unspoken assurance that I was loved. After high school graduation, I left for college in Massachusetts never again to live on Huffman's Cove Road. However, the time I spent on the green hills and sparkling lake with my dear family shaped my life forever.

Makin' Do With Whatcha Got

Millie Kate Huffman Griswold

Seventh and Youngest Child of Arthur and Isma Huffman

It was March 1943 during World War II when Dad came home from working in the shipyard in Norfolk, Virginia. He was unable to work due to severe sciatic rheumatism in his hip and leg. By April, he was on crutches. Dad was 55 years of age. This difficulty would plague him for the next 31 years. The farming was left to Hal, my brother, and Mama. I was 9 years old.

Dad needed some type of productive work. He owned lakefront acreage that sloped into Huffman's Cove. The cove was created in 1928 with backwater from the Catawba River when Duke Power built the Oxford Dam. Dad decided to use the lakefront as a site for docking fishing boats and selling snacks and bait.

Hal helped build a drink stand and boat-docking site close to the bridge on Huffman's Cove Road. Hal had just finished building his first fishing boat. It was agreed that he and Dad would be partners in the

The original concession stand and boat rental was located near the bridge at the end of the cove. It was later moved to deeper water and expanded with a fishing pier that extended two-thirds of the way across Huffman's Cove. Notice in the upper right corner that the barn and chicken house are visible on the east side of the cove adjacent to the homeplace.

fishing business with Hal providing the rental boat. After one year, Hal sold the boat to Dad. It was the only boat Dad ever owned.

Dad spent late afternoons and evenings at the dock where he rented the boat and sold fishing bait, soft drinks, and snacks. During the day, he did farm work as his health permitted. Hal manned the dock on Sunday evenings while Dad and Mama went to church. People living in Hickory brought their boats and launched them from the docking area or left them at the dock for $1.00 per month.

The farm was sown into grass and alfalfa hay. A few cows kept the grass eaten. The heifers born or bought in the spring were sold in the fall for a bit of income.

The spring of 1946, Dad built a fishing pier farther down the river with piers reaching about two thirds of the way across Huffman's Cove. The drink stand from the original dock was moved and placed about thirty feet from the shore at the end of a narrow walkway. Soft drinks, crackers, and peanuts sold for 5 cents each. Bait, minnows, and worms were also for sale.

The pier was sitting on barrels fastened together with heavy coils. There were lights for night fishing and seats around the outside of the pier where fishermen could sit. Dad stayed at the fishing pier from 5:30 to 10:00 p.m. People boating on Lake Hickory would stop by for a drink and crackers or bait.

In 1953, I graduated from high school and left for college in the fall. All seven children were gone from home, but two of them – Allen and Forest—lived within eyesight of the homeplace.

At this point, Dad and Mama were truly living on a "shoe string." Dad's primary income was from the fishing pier and the sale of beef cattle. Money was tight. Dad owned acreage on two hills, but avoided selling it. The fishing pier adjoined one hill, and his house was on the other hill.

All her life, Mama raised a big garden. She canned vegetables and fruit to take us through the winter. A pig and a cow were butchered each fall for meat. A cow or two provided milk and butter. Chickens kept us in eggs and meat. Mama sold butter, eggs, and extra vegetables for her own source of income. In addition, she raised boxwood that she sold to landscapers. She made clothing for herself, for me, and for Granny Mary who lived with us from 1940 to her death in 1958.

Eventually, Dad's health declined so that he could no longer manage the fishing pier. It was time to give up the pier. Mama had a stroke in 1959 and was partially paralyzed.

The Social Security Act passed in 1935, but Dad did not qualify for Social Security since he had not paid into the plan. There was no income. In 1953, Hal agreed to buy the hill adjoining the fishing pier and pay Dad and Mama a yearly amount so they would have income for necessities. The pier closed.

In their final years, Arthur and Isma Huffman lived alone, and between the two of them, they were able to care for each other. Family members helped by bringing in cooked meals. I was the youngest child growing up as my parents' health was in decline. While we lived on the proverbial "prayer and a song," at the time, I didn't know we were poor by today's standards. I was fed, clothed, had a roof over my head, and had a loving family.

Arthur William Huffman was born on March 5, 1888, and he died on July 28, 1974, at 86 years of age. Isma Salome Moretz Huffman was born January 14, 1895, and she died in December 1974 at age 79.

The Damn Dam -- 1928

Mary Mae Huffman

Second Child of Arthur and Isma Huffman

In 1928, Duke Power Company planned to build a dam about 12 miles east of our home. Residents along the Catawba River had mixed feelings about the project. Our farm, along with many other small farms, would be affected since the backwater from the Catawba River would fill up the rich lowlands.

Duke Power was required to purchase the land that would be affected. Some people were willing to sell their property including an additional water right of way; others were not willing to sell.

A small stream ran through our meadow, and Duke Power's maps showed that our choice bottomland would be covered with water. Finally, Dad agreed to sell the water rights.

One night, there was a knock on the door. No one visited after dark unless there was an emergency. When Dad opened the door, there stood our neighbor, Mr. Nance with lantern in hand. He had heard that Duke had given up on the dam business and wanted answers. Dad told him that was untrue. If enough folks agreed to sell their land, Duke could condemn the land of those not wanting to sell.

Mr. Nance was a quiet man. Suddenly he blurted out, "Their dam business is not worth a damn." My brothers and I were a bit shocked because profanity was not allowed in our house. There were a few snickers and Forest, who had a mouthful of cornbread and milk, sprayed the family.

Eventually, all was in order, and the dam construction began. We made one trip to see the "goings on." The dam was completed and water began to fill our meadow. Each morning, we checked to see the progress.

One day, Mama told us that we could swim in the meadow while she watched. (We didn't know how to swim.) We kidded her, "You should come in too." Finally, she waded in and sat down, clothes and all. She stretched out, and we learned that she knew how to float. We laughed ourselves silly.

The backwater that formed Huffman's Cove proved to be a benefit. Through the years, it increased land values, provided recreation, and food when the boys fished using trotlines, baskets, and the annual run of carp up the cove for breeding. In his later years, Dad built a fishing pier, rented boats, and had a concession stand for snacks. This provided a small income.

The damn dam was a blessing.

Note: Mary Mae Huffman wrote this piece as part of a creative writing class she took at the Charlotte YWCA in the 1980's. It provides an additional historical context explaining the creation of Lake Hickory and Huffman's Cove.

Arthur Huffman's Magical Fishing Pier

Kay Huffman Gregory

Daughter of Hal and Rachel Huffman

As I enter her words written long ago into my computer, I can hear my Grandmother's voice quite distinctly. She was a huge presence in our family and in her community while living, and she remains a huge presence in her descendants' lives today. The values that she modeled and instilled in her children and grandchildren survive, rippling out across the waters of time, passing from generation to generation.

In her *Memories Dedicated to My Grandchildren*, Isma Huffman poses this question to her readers: "Did you ever sit down and try to think of the first thing you can remember in your life?" I accepted Isma's challenge. I gave serious thought and dredged through my memories to locate the earliest one. What I recollect is a marvelous concoction of sights and sounds that I experienced sometime during the summer of 1954. I found that early moment in my life perfectly preserved deep in my memories, most likely because it stands out as being markedly different from my daily life as a three-year-old. The details are blurred, but the feelings are sharp.

Hal Huffman and Kay Huffman, 1953.

It was a cool early summer evening. I was traveling over a dirt road with my Daddy in his pickup truck. It was dark, and the tires bumped along hitting ruts left in the road from the last hard rain. The tall weeds that grew in the middle of the road made a swishing noise as they brushed against the bottom of the truck. The scratchy upholstery on the seat was a little rough on my legs, but I was as happy as if I were sitting on a velvet throne. I was on an adventure with my Daddy. Nothing could be better.

Daddy had said that he needed to go see my Grandpa Huffman. He said we were going to the lake. I wasn't sure about the lake part, but I knew who my Grandpa Huffman was. After several curves on the bumpy road, we coasted to a stop.

This photograph shows a busy day at Arthur Huffman's fishing pier. In the upper left corner, the Tabernacle of the Piedmont Youth Camp is visible.

Oh my goodness – the lights! Lights sparkled everywhere in this magical world we had just entered. All along the banks of the lake, lights were strung between poles -- some leaning a little bit to one side, others straight as a ruler. What a pleasure to see these same lights a second time -- twinkling reflections in the lake water.

Daddy told me to hold tight to his hand. We walked down the sloping clay bank of the lake to a narrow wooden walkway strung with more glittering lights. At the end of the walkway was a tiny room with a big opening like a window. Angled pieces of wood held up the slanted little roof that would cover the window opening when it was lowered. Inside the lighted window was my Grandpa, Arthur Huffman. Behind him was a bright red Coca-Cola chest, and the shelves above the drink chest held plastic bags of salted peanuts and cheese crackers. Assorted fishhooks and bait were over to the side. Grandpa smiled with a big smile and joked that I shouldn't fall in because the fish might think I was tasty. I just held on to Daddy's hand a little tighter. This was a beautiful world – the quiet darkness broken only by singing frogs and the occasional lapping water stirred by a breeze. It was also just a little menacing with the mysterious dark waters on all sides. I was thankful for the bright lights that reminded me of Christmas trees.

After Daddy talked a little to Grandpa, he said we would take a walk to the end of the pier. He taught me how to take a big step across the gap between Grandpa's drink stand and the larger, wider fishing pier that seemed to stretch out for miles. He warned me that I should never be careless and fall in that gap because he would have a hard time getting me back. I took that warning very seriously. If the troll from my *Three Billy Goats Gruff* book would have peeked up from the glowing water, I would have not been surprised at all. I just wanted to get past the dangerous part and out to the magical fishing pier illuminated by more lights strung up high with their watery twins floating all around in the water.

Some grownups were sitting quietly at seats scattered all around the pier. They were intently watching their fishing lines that had red and white bobbers floating in the dark water. One man smiled at me and said, "Hey little lady. Where is your fishing pole?" I was a little embarrassed not to have the required equipment for this special world. I told him I didn't know, and that just caused some of the other grownups to laugh. They were friendly, and most of them seemed to know my Daddy. When we got to the far end of the pier, he picked me up and pointed to the darkness. Up high on the dark hill to the right glowed a small yellow light. He said, "That's your Grandma's house. That light is on her porch."

When we turned to walk back toward the drink stand, swarms of pale butterflies were flitting all round the lights. Daddy said they were mayflies. He reached up and caught one so I could take a closer look. When we got to the gaping space between the pier and the drink stand, I was more than happy to remain in Daddy's arms while he confidently stepped across what seemed to me extreme danger. Safely on the other side, we told Grandpa goodbye. Climbing back in the truck, I was sad to leave this special moment, this quiet, light sparkling night on Huffman's Cove.

The waters of the Catawba River figure prominently in the Moretz and Huffman family narratives.

Bicycles, Boats, and Hay Wagons

Dr. Allen William Huffman, Jr.

Son of Allen and Evelyn Huffman

My first memories of Huffman's Cove date from 1946. I arrived at my grandparents' home sitting in the front handlebar basket of my father's bicycle. I was four years old, and my family had just returned from living two years in St. Louis while Dad completed military service.

Allen, Jr. pets a rabbit in St. Louis in 1944.

Mom and Dad rode their bicycles from our home on the dirt Seaboch Road (29th Ave., NE), north two miles on the paved two-lane NC-127 to the dirt Huffman Cove Road (39th Ave. NW). I held on tightly as my father dodged the bumps and holes along the way. I remember the wind in my face as he steered us down the hill and around the curves leading to the long driveway up to Grandpa Huffman's house.

Our pace slowed on the final part of our bicycle ride as we pedaled up the steep drive to the house. A hedge of rose bushes grew on the right side of the drive with a vegetable garden beyond it. On the left side was a low pasture and the public road. The sturdy white, two-story wood frame house sat in the middle of the large hill on the east side of Huffman's Cove. My Dad, Allen, Sr., owned the large hill directly across the road. Grandpa owned three other large hills with pastures that were located on the west side of the Cove.

Dad was not yet able to buy a car in Hickory, but having served in the US Army in 1944-45 as a chaplain's assistant at Jefferson Barracks in St. Louis, he was able to arrange with a St. Louis Chevrolet dealer to get on a new car purchase waiting list by making a down payment. Then in 1947, he rode the train to St. Louis, purchased his new green four-door Chevrolet, and drove back to Hickory.

However, our Sunday afternoon visits continued, and in good weather Grandpa Arthur could be found in his "easy chair" under the great oak trees in the front yard with his dog. Sometimes Aunt Millie or Aunt Mary visiting from Charlotte joined him. Grandma Isma would be hard at work in the kitchen. Often Great-Grandma Mary could be found sitting on the front porch, quietly watching the family gather.

Many pleasant Sunday afternoons were spent enjoying a covered dish lunch under the massive oak trees. This photograph was taken circa 1960.

By 1951, my Dad had built his house on the hill across the road. I had to run down the hill to catch the school bus to ride to Viewmont School, and the first year, I was joined by Aunt Millie who was riding the bus as a senior going to Hickory High School. Later in the 1950's, across Huffman's Cove, Uncle Forest built his house on the north side of Huffman's Cove Road, and Uncle Hal on the south side.

By 1950 Grandpa Arthur had started a fishing business with a small floating store selling snack foods and drinks, as well as fish bait and minnows. He rented boats with oars to fishermen. After a couple of years, he moved down the Cove and enlarged the business to provide a floating fishing pier over the deeper water. The business grew, and many fishermen would bring their own small motors to use with the rental boats. Grandpa hired me to work in the store to sell snacks and drinks. By my high school years, I would run the store alone so that Grandpa could go to the stock sale to buy cattle or do other work. When working with Grandpa, I was paid one dollar a day, but I earned two dollars when working alone. I learned so much about shouldering adult responsibilities from working with Grandpa at the fishing pier. By working alone, I learned to listen and talk to customers about their needs, explain our services, determine the charges, and collect the payment. The fishermen were mill workers from Hickory, farmers from the area, and on weekends some teachers, office workers, and an occasional doctor or banker. After working all day, it felt good to have managed the business for the customers and Grandpa.

One dramatic memory of working at the pier stands out. On a Saturday afternoon, my sister Janice walked over from our house with two cousins. They were playing in the rental boats when Janice fell out into deep water. The cousins were screaming, as was I, when I saw what had happened. Without hesitation, Grandpa Arthur ran down the floating walk way and jumped into the water. He rescued Janice and placed her safely in one of the boats to the relief of cousins, customers, and me. Janice was not allowed to go back to the pier.

In the 1950's and early 1960's Grandpa Arthur continued farming by raising cattle and cutting hay. Grandma Isma continued her vegetable garden work with help from Grandpa as long as he had his horse and

This over-exposed shot of Arthur and Isma's home was taken in 1935 from the eventual house site for Allen and Evelyn Huffman's home.

plow. Even after her stroke, Grandma was sometimes seen running a motor tiller in the garden with one hand.

A crew was hired to cut and bale hay on the flatter hills, but Grandpa cut the steep hill between the house and Cove with the horse drawn riding metal mower. After he raked the hay with the horse drawn rake, my uncles would pitch fork the hay onto the horse drawn wagon. My job was to avoid the pitchforks as I packed the hay with my feet. Grandpa taught me a lot about farming, fishing, animals, and the satisfaction of work well done.

When My World Was New

Dr. Lorene Huffman Painter
Daughter of Cliff and Jennie Huffman
As told to Janet Painter on March 21, 2021

I have the distinction of being Arthur and Isma Huffman's first grandchild, the daughter of their oldest son, Cliff. I was born August 16, 1932. At that time, Arthur and Isma had six of their seven children. Hal, the youngest son, was just four years older than me. Their youngest child, Millie, would be born two years after me. My memories are of the early days that Arthur and Isma Huffman spent in their newly-constructed home sitting on the hill above Huffman's Cove. Lake Hickory itself was still new, the back waters of Oxford Dam covering the bottom meadow in 1928.

I was born just down the road on a farm in what is now Moore's Ferry (the Moore farm). My mother's family were sharecroppers there. As a little girl, I vividly remember Grandma Isma's large vegetable garden, especially picking lots of green beans! Isma milked the cows in the early morning. Much of my grandmother's life revolved around feeding her large family. She canned gallons of vegetables and fruits to provide delicious meals for her family all year long. There were fruit trees on the property that yielded abundant crops for canning and drying.

Grandma Isma's cooking skills were legendary. I remember the large wood-fired cook stove in the kitchen where Isma prepared her delicious baked biscuits and hearty meals like chicken and dumplings. The heat and the smells from that stove were comforting. There was another woodstove in the front room. The boys chopped the firewood, and Isma told them where to put it. The stove in the front room was stoked all day long to warm up the house so that it would remain warm enough on cold nights.

Grandpa Arthur enjoyed socializing with people. He had a fishing pier on Huffman's Cove where he rented boats and sold bait and snacks for the fishermen. I remember that Grandpa was a good hunter, and sometimes, he set traps to catch rabbits for food.

My "Aunt" Millie was actually younger than me, and we had a good time playing together as children. Millie had a bedroom upstairs with windows that looked out over the upper pasture. We often played in her room, and sometimes I got to spend the night with her.

My grandparents worked hard to provide for their family, and they expected their children to work hard as well. The strong work ethic that they modeled in their lives has made a huge impact on my life and the lives of many other people. Grandma Isma always valued education. I have focused my entire career on the field of education, ultimately earning my doctorate degree from UNC-Greensboro and teaching at Lenoir-Rhyne University.

Horace Huffman, Lorene Huffman, and Jerry Huffman, circa 1942.

Suzanne, Jennie, Cliff, and Danny Huffman – circa 1961.

Memories of Arthur and Isma Huffman

Horace Stratford Huffman

Son of Horace Clifton and Jennie Huffman

I am writing down these memories in January 2021. I was born on March 27, 1936. I am now 84 years old. I have been married for 66 years to my wife Peggy Jean Starnes Huffman.

During World War II, I spent a lot of time with Arthur and Isma. Every year in the spring, Grandpa would hook up his horse and wagon and come to our house to plow up our garden. I would ride with him while he plowed. In the fall, I would help pick up sweet potatoes and put them in 60-pound boxes. When I would visit Arthur and Isma's farm, I would help feed the cows, horses, pigs, and chickens.

One day, I wanted to go squirrel hunting. Grandpa Arthur let me use his 16-gauge gun. In two hours, I killed six squirrels and took them to the house. I gave the gun back to him. I was pretty proud of myself!

Arthur had a fishing pier down at the river, and he let me fish anytime I wanted to. Some days I would catch up to fourteen fish. I would take them to Grandma Isma, so she could cook them.

My Aunt Millie Kate was one year older than me. We had many years of fun swimming in Lake Hickory. Then many years later when Grandpa was not able to bathe himself, I would go over and help him take a bath.

I remember how hot it was sleeping upstairs at Arthur and Isma's house in the summer time. There was no air conditioning! Every summer, Arthur and Isma would invite the whole family over to eat ice cream and watermelon. I had a lot of love for both Arthur and Isma and my uncles and aunts. My sweet wife Peggy and I enjoyed visiting everybody – Hal, McCoy, Forest, Allen, Millie Kate, and Mary Mae. I always enjoyed hunting and fishing with my Uncle Hal and Uncle Forest. I enjoyed visiting with them and their wives Rachel and Jeanette as well as my first cousin, Chip Huffman.

Arthur Huffman sitting in his front yard under the two massive oak trees where many family gatherings were held over the years, circa 1965.

Rabbit Meets the Mysterious Girl on the Bus: A Love Story

Jeanette Baker Huffman, Wife of Forest Huffman

as told to

Kay Huffman Gregory

February 11, 2021

I graduated from high school in May 1947. The day after graduation, I was excited to start my new life as an adult. I wanted to travel from my home in Alexander County over to Hickory to go job hunting. I was waiting to catch the bus at Clayton Teague's store at the Highway 127 intersection by the Bethlehem Baptist Church. Clayton Teague said he had to go to MDI over in Hickory, and that he would give me a ride. This was a promising development as it saved me bus fare money.

My maternal grandparents, Avery and Leona Davidson lived in northwest Hickory near Huffman's Cove. They welcomed me to stay at their house where I would be closer to job opportunities in downtown Hickory. I spent the following day looking for jobs all over town. I was fortunate to land a job at Carolina Housing and Mortgage. At that time, they were selling Brookford Mills Housing, and their company handled the financing. In reality, the demands of this job were well beyond the capabilities of a recent high school graduate. I had taken only one course in short hand in high school, and my job was even more challenging due to financial and real estate terms that I had never before encountered.

I worked hard and gave my best effort. Soon, I understood the job requirements. I worked hard to earn my weekly salary of $16. That amount had to cover my clothes, my food, my rent, my transportation – everything!

Each day, I rode the bus to and from work in downtown Hickory. The bus fare was 15 cents each way. At the end of the day, I had to walk across town to below the post office to get to the bus station for the trip home. After a few months, the bus departure point moved to the park on Union Square. This was a bit closer to my job. One afternoon, I caught just a glance of a fellow waiting to get on the bus out to northwest Hickory. I heard someone shout to him, "Hi, Rabbit." It turns out that this fellow was always in a hurry moving quick like a rabbit. I didn't give it much thought. For the next several months, my daily bus rides became a routine.

Then on Halloween night of 1947, there came a knock on Grandma Davidson's door. Grandma said, "Jeanette, someone is here who wants to see you."

I went to the door to find the tall, dark-haired man, the one they called "Rabbit."

"I don't know you," I said. "You must want to see my friend, Jeanette Sigmon. I'll get her."

"No. I want to see you," he insisted. "I have a brand new car. Would you go take a ride with me?"

I said, "No. I don't know who you are."

My grandmother overheard our conversation. She said, "Jeanette, go on with him. I have known his family all my life." It turned out that the Huffmans and the Davidsons were neighbors and farmed adjacent pieces of land for many years. It also turned out that Rabbit couldn't find anyone who knew the mysterious girl he saw riding the bus. He couldn't find anyone to introduce him, so he finally decided on that Halloween night that he would just take the direct approach and knock on the door.

"Well, since Grandma said it would be alright, I will go with you," I relented. I learned that "Rabbit's" real name was Forest Huffman. He asked me where I would like to go. I told him that Mount Olive Lutheran Church was having a Halloween party at a building on the church grounds called "The Hut." He put on a black Halloween mask, and he said we would go.

When we arrived, the other young people wanted to meet my new friend. It turned out that Forest had been dating some of the other girls at the church, so they weren't that happy to see us together. We, however, had a very good time. Forest asked me out for the following Saturday night, but I turned him down since I already had a date scheduled with someone else. That was my last date with anyone other than Forest Huffman!

Back in 1947, we did not have a lot of options for entertainment. Highway 127 was a two-lane paved road. Some Saturday nights, we would go bowling. Other times, we would go roller-skating at the Lakeside Skating Rink located near the Lake Hickory Bridge in Bethlehem. Often, we would end up at Paul's Pork Parlor located close to where the ABC store is now located on Highway 127. I loved going there. I would order a hamburger steak. It was delicious! It is a wonder that they did not throw us out. We would sit in the back with Forest's brother Hal and his date, Rachel Berry. Sometimes James Keller and his date, Mildred Deal, joined us. We would sing real loud and just generally have a very good time.

After Forest and I had been dating for a while, his mother, Isma Huffman, sometimes invited me for her legendary Sunday dinner. The delicious menu was almost always the same. There would be made-from-scratch fresh fried chicken -- as in the chicken was scratching in the yard yesterday! There were green beans and corn preserved from Isma's garden. Steaming rice and yeast rolls were topped with lots of gravy. A homemade cake was served for dessert! An invitation to Isma Huffman's table was not a meal to miss! Her dining room table had eight chairs. She wanted all eight filled each Sunday at lunch, and if young children filled the kitchen table, that was OK as well. I learned all about Forest's brothers and sisters from those Sunday afternoons spent at his home.

On Thanksgiving of 1947, I did not have transportation to return to my parents' home for the holiday. I was still working at Carolina Housing and Mortgage with a young woman named Merna Moretz. She invited me to come to her home for Thanksgiving. At the time, I did not realize that she and Forest were first cousins.

Merna's father, Carl Moretz, was Isma Moretz Huffman's younger brother. Merna tried to explain to me how Forest's parents – Arthur and Isma -- were both husband and wife as well as stepbrother and stepsister. Well, that was a difficult concept for me. But I finally understood. Arthur's father, Daniel Huffman, was a widower. Isma's mother, Mary Moretz, was a widow. They married each other after their children were grown, a second marriage for both. Arthur had been working out in Wyoming for several years, and his father remarried while he was away. When Arthur returned home, he fell in love with one of his stepsisters, Isma. They had no blood relationship, and they met each other as young adults.

Forest and Jeanette with the silver gray '47 Chevrolet, circa 1948.

As time passed, Forest would pick me up after work more and more in that silver gray 47 Chevrolet. I loved seeing my handsome boyfriend, and

I appreciated not having to spend 15 cents to ride the bus. I remember on one Sunday, there was a big snow. I had walked to Mount Olive Lutheran Church without snow boots. My cousin Russell Smith's children, Gary Dean and Gloria, wanted to come home to Grandma Davidson's with me. As we walked home in the snow, we were throwing snowballs at each other. Just as we were getting wet and cold, Forest drove up in his car and took us home. That car sure came in handy!

One day Forest told me he was going to come over and see me at Grandma Davidson's that evening. I told him not to come because I had to iron. I was ironing when I heard a knock on the door. Forest came any way just to watch me iron. I guess we were getting more and more love struck. For Christmas 1947, Forest asked his brother Hal to locate a radio to give me. Hal found a nice one that included not just a radio but a 78-rpm record player as well. That radio and record player are still down in my basement, and they both still work! For my birthday in February 1948, Forest gave me a string of Marvella pearls that were knotted between each pearl. I was so proud of that beautiful necklace.

The next thing I knew, we were engaged to be married. I am so glad that my Grandma Davidson nudged me to go out on that first date with Forest. Had she not given her recommendation for Forest, I might not be telling this story. On June 5, 1948, our wedding was held at Mount Olive Lutheran Church. We were married for 68 ½ years until Forest's death on November 23, 2016. All of my experiences shared here tell how I came to be a part of one of the most wonderful families in the world -- the Arthur and Isma Huffman family.

Precious Memories

Daniel Frederick Huffman

Son of Clifton and Jennie Huffman

I have fond memories of the holiday gatherings and meals at the Grandpa and Grandma Huffman house overlooking Huffman's Cove. I will get to the food later, but my best memories are the cousins, aunts, uncles, and grandparents. I was always excited to see the family together and to play with my cousins and receive special attention from aunts and uncles not seen for months and sometimes years.

Grandmother Huffman was a good cook and never disappointed her family on these special days. Even after a debilitating stroke, she continued to prepare the holiday meals. Before the meals, there was always a blessing either by Grandpa or if a preacher was present by the preacher. I will list a few of my food memories, but the list is certainly not all-inclusive. Roast fat chicken hen and sometimes turkey with delicious dressing, deviled eggs, baked ham, roast beef, creamed corn, green beans, cranberry sauce or salad, gelatin salad, yeast rolls (homemade), baked apples, creamed rice, potato salad, and always gravy.

Desserts included hoover cake, fruitcake, sugar cookies with candied fruit, black walnut cookies, coconut cake, red velvet cake, apple pie, rhubarb strawberry pie, pecan pie, and always ice cream and whipped cream. Most of the foods were home grown right there on the farm and pulled from the freezer or canning jar. The chickens, ham, and beef were all home grown.

After the meal, there was always piano playing, carol singing at Christmas, tall tales, and socializing. The cameras then came out, and the photos are priceless today. The house, barns, car garage, gardens, boxwoods, and chicken houses are all gone, but the memories remain. Precious memories.

Cousins -- Kay, Allen Jr., Janice, Suzanne, and Danny Huffman, 1953.

Memories of My Younger Years

"Chip" -- Hal Franklin Huffman, Jr.

Son of Hal and Rachel Huffman

I have many memories with Grandpa and Grandma Huffman beginning when I was 3-6 years old (pre-school years). My day would start with walking from the house where I now live to the opposite hill across Huffman Cove to spend the day with Arthur and Isma while my parents worked. Grandpa always started his day milking the two to three Jersey cows. He felt it was his mission to teach me to milk. It would always start out with him squirting milk on my shoes as a game to rope me in and finish with me actually doing the milking. This was an everyday event. Through the course of the day, I would follow Grandpa around the property while he performed his daily tasks -- feeding and watering the cows, working in the garden if it were summer, picking up apples in the orchard, gathering eggs for Grandma, or chasing a chicken through the yard to kill for lunch. I'm sure you all remember the diamond shaped holes in the stables of the barn and what Grandpa used one of them for.

When he slaughtered a chicken, he had a chop block outside the stable. He would chop off the chicken's head holding him by the legs and stuffing him inside the hole to let him bleed out inside the stable, a very efficient and clean process.

Grandma always had fresh homemade biscuits for lunch with her homemade butter, and I always looked forward to that part of the meal. We always had fresh vegetables from the garden or vegetables that had been canned for the winter. She would always have meat such as chicken, pork, or beef, and sometimes a few things that were definitely not my favorite. I might walk into the kitchen and find a cow tongue boiling in the pot or pig's feet or beef liver. The beef liver had a very distinct smell, which made me nauseated. They would always do their best to see that I had a taste of everything put in front of me.

Every Thursday was Stock Sale Day, and if I was there, Grandpa would always take me with him. The Stock Sale at that time was located where the new Hickory High School is now sitting. When we arrived, Grandpa would always make his way around the holding pens to see what kind of livestock had been brought to market that day. When the sale started, we would sit up in the wooden stands surrounding the sale pen while Charles Ray Yount, the Auctioneer and one of Grandpa's nephews, would call out the sale for each animal. As a child, I was fascinated with the speed of his speech, and it took me a long while to figure out what he was saying except when he hollered out "Sold" to whomever made the purchase. Once I was leaning over the rail into the sale pen trying to pet 4 or 5 goats that were tied in the corner. I leaned over too far and fell directly into the sale pen on top of the goats. Unscathed but scared, I was rescued by one of the sale hands who lifted me back over the rail, and everyone present had a good laugh. Charles Ray said I would bring a good price if he auctioned me off.

Some of my fondest memories came from sitting with Grandpa in the front yard under the big oak trees in the old sling back chairs that were Grandpa's favorite. He would spend hours telling me stories of his Wyoming Cowboy days. As you all know, he was foreman of a cattle operation on an Indian Reservation outside Riverton, Wyoming. One story he told was when he had to ride horseback two days to a dentist to have an abscessed tooth taken care of. I heard many stories of the Indians and their way of life. Just about daily, he would do Indian chants that he learned while on the reservation. If you heard them today, you would think they were made up. But his chants and memories of life on the reservation were real.

Four years after Grandma and Grandpa were married, Grandpa's adventurous spirit wanted to return to Wyoming. His plan was to work out there long enough to pay for their land on Huffman's Cove. This time he would journey to Wyoming with his wife and two young children – Cliff age three and one half and Mary Mae age two. Once they arrived by train at Riverton, Wyoming, they still had a two-day wagon trip across the prairie to get to Lander. When I watched the mini-series *Lonesome Dove* on TV, I thought Grandpa and Gus (Robert Duvall) were of the same mind.

Grandpa considered himself a great horseman. He made certain that I would know how to ride a horse. Everyday we would go to the mailbox to get the mail and the *Hickory Daily Record*. If it were not raining, he would get Tamarack out of the pasture and lead me riding bareback to the mailbox. At the bottom of the drive was a large ditch that he made me jump every time we went down the drive. In the beginning, I cried and screamed. Later that became the highlight of the walk. Once he took me on a long horseback lead through the woods on the old Whisnant Property where Moore's Ferry is now located. We walked some of the horse trails to the old Cemetery. At my young age, the cemetery was a scary place. He also found a patch of wild strawberries, and we ate them as well as feeding them to Tamarack.

Grandpa was also obsessed with moving cattle from one pasture to another. Just about weekly, we would move cows from his pasture around the house to the pasture across the cove at the camp. He would put me up front with a feed bucket, which I could barely carry, to coax the cows down the drive and roadway. He would bring up the rear with his walking cane and collie dog. If things did not go just right, he would hurl his walking cane at cows not following the herd and always used his favorite word, "SHIT! Chip, keep moving." I would always be struggling to keep three or four cows from putting their big wet noses in the feed bucket and stopping my forward motion, which disrupted the whole process.

Grandpa was also a man of few words. When he spoke, it had meaning, so you did well to listen to every word. If you spoke to Grandpa on the phone, you better not pause during the conversation. With just a moment of silence during the call, with no hesitation or goodbye, he would hang up the phone assuming the conversation was over.

From my first memory of Grandpa and Grandma, I never noticed a change in their physical appearance. Grandpa was 66 years old when I was born in 1954, so he was always old in my eyes. I never really knew the young Arthur Huffman. When Grandpa passed in 1974, I was the one who answered the phone at the hardware when the caregiver called and said Grandpa had collapsed at the breakfast table. He was having his morning coffee sipped from a saucer (to cool it off), had a heart attack, and fell over backwards onto the floor -- an abrupt end. If only we all could go out that easy at 86 years old.

Unfortunately I have many more stories and memories with Grandpa than I do with Grandma. Grandma, due to her stroke, was not able to roam the Huffman Cove hills like Grandpa and I did, so our interactions were not as consistent throughout the day. One of my favorite activities with her was pressing butter in the wooden butter molds she had. I helped her string beans, silk corn, snap peas, and various other canning duties. I thought it was really cool to roll out the bread dough covered with flour using her wooden rolling pin and then to cut out the biscuits with a round cutter. I remember her as a very kind woman and extremely strong willed. As much as Grandpa thought he was in control, she really ran the ship, and he followed.

The biggest thing I took away from spending time with Grandpa and Grandma were values that have stayed with me throughout my life. Arthur and Isma both modeled an extremely strong work ethic. As Grandpa often said, "Hard work never hurt anybody." Likewise, they insisted on strong morals and put their religious faith in action. They raised their children with very simple guidelines: "Don't cheat, don't lie, and don't steal. Be honest. Do what's right. Love your family. Remember that life is short!" The seven Huffman children instilled those same values in their children as well. Thus, Arthur and Isma remain a force influencing future generations.

Arthur William Huffman, circa 1963.

The Cuckoo Clock

Scott Christopher Huffman

Son of McCoy and Louise Huffman

When I was nine or ten years old, I loved going down to Grandma and Grandpa's house. They had a cuckoo clock that always fascinated me. When no one was around, I'd climb up on something and try to catch the cuckoo when it came out. I did this about every time we visited.

On one occasion, I actually grabbed the tiny bird when it came out. I was so proud of myself for being able to grab it until I turned around and right behind me stood Grandpa. He didn't spank me, but let me tell you, I got a lecture and scolding I never forgot. To this day, if I think of Grandpa and Grandma, I think of that cuckoo clock.

Salt in the Wound

Joy Griswold Gallagher
Daughter of Roland & Millie Huffman Griswold

Grandpa always had wonderful stories to tell of when he worked out West in Wyoming. I loved that fact that MY Grandpa had been a real cowboy. One of his favorite places to sit seemed to be outside under the tree at the side of the house. When I was younger, I couldn't understand why he would just want to **sit**, but as I joined him, I began to appreciate the stillness. I heard the birds singing, the cows munching in the pasture, and occasionally the thump of a golf ball landing in the yard when Uncle Allen was hitting them from his yard across the road and over the hill. I loved listening to Grandpa do the Native American chants and the stories he would tell of helping on the reservation.

One summer Grandpa taught me to whittle under that big tree. I watched for a while as he talked to me about what he was doing; then, I got a chance. I was so proud of the fact that he let me use his jackknife, and I thought I was doing a pretty good job of learning this new-found skill. Grandpa had to go in the house for a minute and said he would be right back; he also told me to not whittle anymore until he returned.

Well . . . I didn't listen. I guess I wanted to make him proud of what he had taught me, so I picked up the knife and started to whittle. There was one problem. I was using the knife on the stick whittling ***towards*** me, not away from me. I ended up slicing the thumb of the hand holding the stick! It was bleeding -- bleeding a lot. I went inside screaming! Grandpa didn't fuss at first. He put my hand over the sink in the kitchen and had Grandma give him the big bag of salt.

He plunged my bleeding finger into the bag of salt. I was hollering because it stung so badly, and I was shocked at how quickly the salt was turning red. He took my hand out of the salt, rinsed it off, dried it, investigated, and then plunged that thumb back into the salt. He had me sit at the kitchen table with my thumb in the salt bag for what seemed like forever. Eventually he took it out, cleaned it off, and bandaged it.

Then I got a tongue lashing (which I deserved) for disobeying. The thumb stung for a long time that day. I was not able to go swimming in the lake with my cousins for a week; we couldn't chance infection. Grandpa had learned about using salt to stop bleeding from his father, Daniel the veterinarian. The interesting thing was the deep cut where I had tried to filet my thumb healed quicker than anyone thought it would, and there was no scar! As much as I hated the sting of the salt, it was a great lesson in the consequences of disobedience AND the healing power of salt. I have used that remedy many times with my family. We may have winced at the salt sting, but are always amazed at the rapid healing.

Grandma's Kitchen

Melodie Lee Griswold

Daughter of Roland and Millie Kate Huffman Griswold

I have many memories of my Grandma Isma Huffman in the kitchen. She really seemed to love cooking and watching others enjoy what she had prepared. In my mind, I can still see each wall of the busiest room in that home. There were windows along the wall above the kitchen sink, and so the kitchen was usually filled with lots of light. Along this wall is where much food preparation took place. The countertop was a silver metal worn dull with years of daily use. I remember the pull out flour bin she had. I had never seen anything like that before. It was integrated into the cabinetry, and I imagine that it would hold at least 25 pounds of flour, enough for a woman who spent her life cooking for large numbers of people.

I also remember her singing "Surely goodness and mercy shall follow me all the days of my life" as she made biscuits. She was such a happy cook! Many folks today are reluctant and cook from duty, but Grandma cooked with love. At the far end of the kitchen was a doorway out onto the large screened-in back porch. The kitchen had a nice flow and was designed for efficiency, but always had an aura of warmth. I remember sitting on the porch with Grandma, Mom, Aunt Mary, my sister, and my cousins, popping green beans, shucking corn, and hand preparing some of the vegetable crops for canning.

After seeing the close-up drama of a chicken slaughtered and then featured as fried chicken for supper, all proteins were suspect for a while. I was afraid the country style steak was a cow I had seen in the pasture earlier. I was not accustomed to the circle of life. I was also afraid to drink chocolate milk with white bits floating around in it; I didn't know it was the wholesome milk fat.

Apparently, Grandma's love of cooking was passed down through generations, as my mother, my sister, and I all enjoy cooking and sharing the results. We enjoy making some of her recipes, including chicken and dumplings (Southern style "go-slick" dumplings made with strips of dough), wilted spinach salad with bacon dressing, biscuits and sausage gravy, and of course, that country style steak.

Joyce and Melodie Griswold, circa 1963.

The Sweetest Love

Amanda Isma Huffman Hall
Daughter of Hal and Rachel Huffman

On January 23, 1961, a daughter was born to Hal and Rachel Huffman. They named me Amanda Sue. A few years later, my name was changed to Amanda Isma Huffman. I have no memory of this event as the official date is January 12, 1965, a few weeks shy of my fourth birthday. My oldest sister Kay, 14 at the time, does remember overhearing conversations between our parents as they made the decision to legally change my name. As I got older, I realized the significance and honor of bearing the name of our remarkable Grandma Huffman, Isma Salome Moretz Huffman.

I treasure the varied memories of time spent with Grandma and Grandpa Huffman. During the school year, Grandma and Grandpa would keep me on days that Mom had to work. Kay, Chip and Beth were already in school at Viewmont Elementary and College Park Junior High. I also was in school - a school where Arthur and Isma taught me lessons about being a good person, helping others, and about the importance of hard work and a job done right. I also learned the joy of a walk in the woods.

Mom would drop me off at Grandma's early after breakfast. I would usually find Grandpa sitting in his chair right inside the door from the side porch. Grandma would be finishing up breakfast chores in the kitchen and starting lunch if it required a long cook. I would always sneak a peek in the pot, hoping for anything other than cow tongue! Grandma usually had a leftover dish for me from the night before if cow tongue was on the menu. Plus, we always had hot biscuits and butter.

Grandma made me feel very important in the kitchen. Her tactic also got a lot of work out of me! Nothing would make me feel more proud than a word of praise for a job well done from Grandma. I was the dishwasher. Grandma would pull up a ladder-back chair to the counter, fill the sink with hot soapy water, and pile up the dirty dishes ready for me to wash. On one occasion I remember, there was a Pyrex with a lot of cooked on grease. I worked and worked on that dish until it was shiny clean. Grandma made a point of telling my mom what good kitchen help I was that day. I was beaming ear to ear. I imagine Mom was wondering how to get such results out of me at home.

Another favorite memory in Grandma's kitchen was making popcorn balls. In my memory, this was always a Halloween treat. First we would pop a big batch of corn and set that aside. Then Grandma would take a large cast-iron frying pan, melt some grease and add molasses to heat. She would then stir and add water until the mixture was "a hairing." That was the term she used to describe the look of the molasses when you held a spoonful of hot molasses high over the pan. Grandma would give the spoon a slight tilt and the molasses mixture drizzled out in a narrow stream, thin like a strand of golden hair. When the molasses was "a hairing," it was time to pour it over the popcorn. Then my job began which was to stir the mixture and form it into balls before it set up too hard. This was tricky because that molasses was hot! I had to work fast.

Most days when I stayed with Grandma and Grandpa Huffman, after lunch and a little nap, Grandpa and I would take a walk. I am sure we were quite a sight. There would be Grandpa, posture straight as an arrow, walking with his cane. I would be following along chattering the whole way. Ben the collie dog would be keeping pace with us or ranging ahead. And then strolling somewhere not too far behind us would be Ringtail the cat. We would walk down their gravel drive and cross over Huffman's Cove Road towards Uncle Allen's driveway. Then we would walk just above his drive towards what is now Moore's Ferry. Right in the big curve, we would veer right into the woods and go "exploring." I always loved the walks. Grandpa would tell stories about things he had done or teach me about the various plants and trees that we would pass by. We returned back to the house refreshed and with the day's mail.

Sometimes I was lucky enough to take a trip to the store with Grandma and Grandpa. We would get in Grandpa's huge blue car and head to the Fresh Air Supermarket. I think Grandpa stayed in the car because I only remember pushing the buggy through the aisles with Grandma. Occasionally, but not every trip, she would send me down the ice cream aisle looking for Pet Dairy Brown Mules. Grandma claimed that was her favorite ice cream. At the time I thought "wow, mine too!" I do think Grandma liked Brown Mules, because we would get home and sit in the kitchen each eating one. Now I realize that the special treat was for me. I have looked over the years for Brown Mules, but can never find

Amanda Isma Huffman, age 9, visits Isma and Arthur on their side porch overlooking Huffman's Cove.

them. Mayfield Dairies has a Black Cow Ice Cream, but it is just not the same.

Let's go back to Grandpa's car and his unusual driving style. While Grandma was getting ready to go, Grandpa and I would go to the car shed. I would crawl into the back seat, and Grandpa would back the car out and go pick up Grandma in the yard by the porch off the kitchen. Any of us who have ridden with Grandpa will remember his steering technique! He held his hands in a steady 4:00 and 8:00 position on the steering wheel. He shimmied the steering wheel between his hands in the needed direction of an approaching curve or turn. That was a lot of quick movements for a sharp turn! As I got older, I realized this unique driving style was due to Grandpa's arthritic pain and stiffness.

Upon returning home, Grandpa would again pull the car up near the kitchen porch. I would unload the groceries, hop back into the car in the front seat and ride with Grandpa back to the car shed. He always made a game of pulling in fast, joking that we might just drive straight through the back of the shed and end up in the lake! We never did, of course. But to a 5 or 6 year old, even then, that car shed was sketchy hanging out over the pasture like it did.

Grandpa Huffman was a bit of prankster. I liked to follow Grandpa around the barn, helping with chores if I could. Grandpa got a kick out of squirting our shoes with milk when he was milking their cow. I remember the time he squirted my brand new pair of saddle oxfords. That was the last time he got my shoes wet! I learned to keep a safe distance from the milking stool. Another job with Grandpa was skinning the occasional squirrel. My job was to hold the squirrel by his hind legs, while Grandpa got to the business of cleaning it. While I was squeamishly doing my part, Grandpa would do his, laughing the whole time. I can hear his voice, insisting "now hold him, hold him still."

As I got older and started school, visits fell to the weekends or evenings. For many summers my sister Beth and I would mow Grandma and Grandpa's yard. When you let your mind wander over the yard, you'll remember it was a big yard! We each would take a one-hour turn pushing Grandpa's heavy mower over the yard. I can remember mowing along the side of the house towards the upper field and waving at

Grandma through the kitchen window. It would take a full day to get the job done, and we each got $5 a piece for our effort.

I have so many snippets of memories too numerous to share here - Snowball the big white cat, Ben and Laddie the collie dogs, the beautiful hydrangea bushes and boxwood around Grandma and Grandpa's house, and all the outbuildings to explore and incorporate into the imaginative games of young children. In my mind, I like to walk through their house, trying to remember the rooms, the furniture and what was hanging on the walls. I think about the few times I went down into what can only be called the root cellar off the kitchen, such a scary and cool place at the same time! There was a small telephone cubby right in the wall of the stairwell leading upstairs with no chair nearby to sit and have a conversation in comfort. Of course, long telephone conversations were not a common occurrence for Grandma and Grandpa. One of my favorite memories is how Grandma, sitting in her chair by the window, would have conversations with me just like an adult. She told me once she had read the entire dictionary and had read their set of encyclopedias. I believe her. She was a smart lady.

Above all else, what I remember about Grandma and Grandpa Huffman was feeling so loved at their house. Walking into their home felt warm and safe to me. I'm sure I was scolded at their house, but I don't remember it! Both Grandma and Grandpa were quick to smile and laugh. I love to revisit those precious sights and sounds. Their lives were full of hard work to survive - Grandma's book proves that point. And at the same time, their lives were dedicated to their church and service to others. They modeled integrity and positivity. That is what I hold onto as the most lasting legacy of Arthur and Isma Huffman.

"Nobody can do for little children what grandparents do.
Grandparents sort of
sprinkle stardust over the lives of little children."

~Alex Haley

Isma Salome Moretz Huffman, circa 1963.

Grandma and the Jehovah's Witnesses

Kay Huffman Gregory
Daughter of Hal and Rachel Huffman

From time to time, members of the Jehovah's Witnesses would visit homes on Huffman's Cove Road. My mother would never let the strangers into our home. She would politely tell them that she had a church family and that she had no interest in changing her religious affiliation. She would firmly send them on to their next stop.

One afternoon, I was over at Grandma and Grandpa Huffman's home when a lady and a man from the Jehovah's Witnesses knocked on Grandma Isma's door. Grandma Isma graciously invited them inside. The lady asked Grandma if she could share some scripture with her. Grandma agreed, but at the same time she reached for her Bible. Oh, this is going to be interesting, I thought. Grandma knew her Bible. She taught Bible study classes and Sunday school. Around her chair in the den, there were always books of scriptural analysis stacked on the floor.

After the woman's scripture reading, Grandma seemed to like the scripture but not the woman's interpretation of it. She said, "Now I want to read a scripture to you." She then proceeded to tell the woman her Advent Christian view of the situation. The woman smiled and asked if she could read another passage. What transpired over the next several minutes was like a Bible Sword Drill we once did at Youth Fellowship. It was fascinating.

Back and forth, the two women politely debated – neither actually giving any ground. At one point, Grandma asked me to get everyone a glass of iced tea. She said, "Kay, these good people are bound to be thirsty." I thought to myself, "Yep. Anyone who debates the Bible with Isma Huffman is going to be thirsty alright." That afternoon, I learned a great deal about civil discourse. I have never forgotten the respect that those two Christian women showed each other. They parted cordially.

As surely as the sun rose each morning, Isma and Arthur Huffman sat in "their" pew at the First Advent Christian Church. Their seats were located on the fourth row back from the front of the church. There, they anchored the far left side of that pew every Sunday morning. Their regular attendance and participation in church activities was a wonderful model for others. However, I learned even more about the value of a strong moral compass by watching Arthur and Isma as they navigated daily life on Huffman's Cove. They both lived their faith.

My Hero

Melodie Lee Griswold

Daughter of Roland and Millie Kate Huffman Griswold

I always loved to hang out with my grandpa, Arthur Huffman, when we came to visit. Farm life on Huffman's Cove was very different from what I experienced daily at the various urban places my family lived over the years such as Plainville, Connecticut; Detroit, Michigan; and Charlotte, North Carolina. I really enjoyed spending time with him outdoors, and I loved experiencing life on a farm. I always looked forward to walking the pastures and watching him complete jobs such as milking the cows. He always gave me a walking stick, and he also used one. That was fun. Some of the walking sticks were quite decorative. One was made from a small limb that had a vine growing in a spiral fashion around it, and the growth of the vine left a spiral in the wood of the walking stick.

Grandpa had collie dogs, and one of them always walked around with him. I loved dogs too, and I sure enjoyed the dog coming along. I remember Grandpa trying to teach me how to milk a cow, which wasn't successful but certainly was interesting. He would make milking look so

Arthur Huffman disk harrowing the field above the house, circa 1940.

easy, but every time I tried to squeeze, I wasn't doing it quite right and no milk came out. I really loved following him around all day. We walked the pastures to check on the cows, and walked all around the property to assure all the animals were okay, fences were in place, and nothing needed repair.

I remember one time when we went to a livestock sale, and I think he was considering getting a pony because he knew how much I loved horses. My dad quickly dissuaded him from that. However, it was fun going and watching the bidding on the animals. Observing the crowd and listening to the fast-paced voice of the auctioneer was a totally new experience for me.

I also remember grandpa talking about the Indians and singing some of their songs. As a young man, grandpa had gone out West to Wyoming, and for a while, he worked as ranch foreman for an Indian School for girls. He got to learn some of the Indian culture. It was really cool to hear him singing Indian songs and chants. They sure sounded authentic to me.

Sometimes Grandpa would take my big sister Joy and me to the local convenience store. Grandpa called these trips "going to Arizona." That was one of his jokes that never got old. Once inside, he would let us get one item, whatever we wanted.

I always looked forward to visiting Huffman's Cove and spending time with grandpa and my cousins.

Isma and Arthur are ready for church, circa 1955.

Monkeys in the Rafters

Beth Huffman

Daughter of Hal and Rachel Huffman

As a child, I spent many hours at Grandma and Grandpa Huffman's home. Some of my best memories were made in their magical barn overlooking Huffman's Cove. It was a well-built structure with every square inch of the barn serving a functional purpose – shelter, storage, protection, breeding, and milking. I spent endless hours playing in the nooks and compartments. It was an enchanting, scary, entertaining, and genially designed structure where grandkids spent summer afternoons hanging from the rafters like monkeys.

There was a covered open-air area on the front side of the barn where you could tie up a horse to saddle it. As I remember, beyond the upper door there was a storage area and stable to the left. Straight ahead was a ladder to an upper loft where hay and straw were stored for the animals. The lower level provided large stables for the livestock, and there were three compartments – a large area entered through a lower level door, a smaller pen in the left corner of the barn and then a larger area to the

This silk-screened image of the barn at Huffman's Cove created by Ken Gregory evokes many fond memories for the children who played there.

right. Gates connected all the stables so the livestock could be moved around as needed. Ladders were built to provide access to the three levels of the barn. I remember vividly that the diamond shaped openings near the front of the barn were not for architectural purposes, but for the chickens to spend their final moments before heading to Grandma's kitchen for lunch.

Inside the lower level, we got to milk cows with Grandpa. He would sit on an overturned bucket and milk into a big galvanized pail. The barn cats would gather around so as not to miss the occasional splash of milk that Grandpa would send their way. He let us help milk the cow each time we visited. As a child, I focused on the technique, but I was keenly aware of the size of the cow and those big hoofs that could move my way at any moment. Thankfully, the cows always cooperated.

In the winter months when the grass was sparse, we were allowed to feed hay to the cows from the hayloft. You could hear the cows munching on the hay with those enormous teeth, and it was a good reminder not to disturb them at feeding time. Sometimes they came inside the barn, and other times we threw the bales into the pasture behind the barn. When it rained, we threw straw out on the ground to prevent the barn area from being so muddy.

The grandkids played hide and seek in the barn, and occasionally we ran into some unwelcome furry creatures that called the barn home. There was the occasional snake or two that we encountered, and they weren't any happier to see us than we were to see them.

The livestock that lived in the barn provided food for the family, as well as providing income. In the spring, Grandpa bought cows at the Hickory Livestock Sale, and they grazed on the pasture all summer. Usually in the fall, they butchered a cow and froze the meat for the winter. Some of the other cows were sold at a profit after they matured from the benefit of the lush pasture all summer. The chickens laid eggs, and Grandma always had fresh eggs to eat and to share. Grandma wasn't bashful about catching a chicken for the next meal, and she was quite accurate with a hatchet. As I remember, there was always something good cooking on her kitchen stove, and her chicken and dumplings topped the list for me. I would always crawl up on a stool to look inside the big pots to see what was cooking. The only time it shocked me was when I lifted the pot lid and saw a cow tongue boiling on the stove.

Obviously, there was no waste, and they used all of their resources to feed the family.

Still today, I can close my eyes and see the inside of the barn on Huffman's Cove. I fondly cherish the memories made there.

In 1954, Arthur and Isma are in their living room in the left picture. The right picture is taken in their den area in 1972.

Snapshots of Grandmother Isma and Grandpa Arthur

Joy Griswold Gallagher
Daughter of Roland & Millie Huffman Griswold

I did not grow up near Grandma and Grandpa Huffman; however, we spent 2-3 weeks each summer at their house. My Dad would often drive us there and stay a few days, and then would go back to whatever church he was pastoring. Mom, Melodie, and I would stay a few weeks, and then Dad would come back and get us. Because Melodie and I lived away from the rest of the family, I always looked forward to the times when I had cousins to play with. My memories are more snapshots in time, but they bring great joy to my heart.

I remember the flower planters that Grandma had by the front steps of the house. They had some kind of bushy rose, I think, in them and they were always beautiful. I remember watching her work in the garden. Sometimes she would "make" us come help her. Even though I did not enjoy the hard work, I loved seeing things grow and her diligence in hoeing because she wanted to provide good things for her family. I even

Cousins gather with Grandma Isma. Front left to right: Beth Huffman, Melodie Griswold, Amanda Huffman, Joy Griswold. Back: Barry Huffman, Lisa Bradford, Mary Mae Huffman, and Isma Huffman, circa 1968.

remember her taking the hoe and limping to the garden after she had recovered from her stoke. She found a way to get there and to hoe because she loved it; I think that garden was her sanctuary.

I remember the butter churn on the back porch and the beautifully decorated pounds of butter she sold to people in the community. I don't know what happened to those butter molds. I have never seen any like them. The back porch was where I remember helping process the produce from the garden. I also remember the chest freezer that sometimes held homemade ice cream in a 9 X 13 pan.

I loved Grandma's kitchen and loved watching her cook. The big flour bin and the steel counter top were absolutely perfect for all of the cooking she did. Her yeast rolls were perfection. I loved when we got to have Sunday dinner in the dining room. I always felt so "fancy" and the food was always delicious. The sewing machine was kept in that room. I learned to sew one summer using that machine. Grandma and Mom had a lot of patience as they helped me make Barbie doll clothes. As an adult I am amazed as I remember that Grandma designed that house. The detail and thought put into every room was amazing.

Melodie, Mom and I usually stayed in the bedrooms upstairs. I always got the room on the backside of the house that faced the pasture. I loved hearing the rooster and seeing the cows out the bedroom window. Some days I would wake up and pretend I was Rebecca of Sunny Brook Farm. I recall nights when there were storms, and Melodie and I would be afraid. Mom would come up and rock Melodie to sleep in one room, and I could hear her singing lullabies that soothed both of us. I have sung those songs to my children and now to my grandson. My kids laugh and call "Kentucky Babe" the "Mimi Magic" because whenever I rock my grandson, Jonathan, and sing that song, he falls asleep.

I loved the piano in the parlor. Once I got where I could play hymns, there were days I would open the hymnbook, start at the beginning and play hymn after hymn until I got tired of playing. Grandma and Grandpa were very gracious because I am sure the sounds coming from the piano were not always sweet. When Aunt Mary would come from Charlotte for the weekend, she would stay in the bedroom that was off of the parlor. There were times I would have to sleep with her. The joke was that we wanted to go to bed and be asleep before Aunt Mary went to bed or we would never get sleep for her snoring.

The living room was where I recall spending most of my time. There wasn't a lot of seating, but it was sufficient. I loved the wooden built in bookcase in that room. Grandpa had a special jar with the most amazing peppermint sticks in it. You knew you were loved when he pulled that jar out and gave you one, but don't you ever sneak in there and take one yourself. The phone was in that room. I don't remember using it that much, but I do recall that one summer my parents left me and Melodie with Grandma and Grandpa for 3 weeks while they went to a denominational convention. We knew where they were going, Aurora College in Illinois, I think. I recall mailing a letter that Mom saved. After about 2 weeks, Melodie and I were really missing them. I somehow found the phone number, and when no one was in the house, I proceeded to make the long distance call. Whoever answered the phone had to track down my parents before I could even talk to them. I don't remember whether Mom or Dad got on the phone. I do know I was in BIG trouble for the large long distance phone bill.

I loved the farm, but wasn't fond of the barn; I was always afraid I would come across a snake. Grandpa did his best to try and teach Melodie and me how to milk a cow. We weren't very good at it. Melodie and I were outside one time when Grandpa was getting ready to kill a chicken. He had us watch and talked to us about what he was doing. What he forgot to tell us was that the chicken might run around for a bit even once its head was cut off. Melodie and I ran and screamed because we thought the chicken was chasing us. I remember there was always at least one collie at the house; I loved to brush them.

Grandma and Grandpa's bedroom was off the living room. There were 2 beds and a wooden table that had lots of medicine bottles and sometimes a vase with flowers. Their 50th Anniversary party was held at their house; unfortunately, I don't remember anything about it. I didn't feel well, so Mom had me lay down on one of the beds in their room. I fell asleep and didn't wake up until long after the party had ended.

I don't remember what kind of car Grandpa had; I just remember it was long, and he parked it in a garage, of sorts. He sometimes kept the windows in it down, and there might be a dirt dobber nest on the roof inside. Grandpa would sometimes ask us if we wanted to go to "Wyoming" or "Arizona" -- I guess from his cowboy days. We knew that meant we were either going to Hutto's store and could get candy, or somewhere to get ice cream. My dad continued that tradition with my girls, and we plan to continue it with our grandson.

After her stroke, Grandma had her brain surgery at a hospital in Charlotte. My family lived in the Charlotte area at that time, and I remember going to the hospital to visit with her several times a week. I would bring a brown mule, her favorite ice cream, and she would ask me to read the Bible to her. It could be any passage I wanted on some days, but most days her request was Romans 8. If she was strong enough when I got to certain verses, she would recite them as I was reading; when her strength was failing, she would just mouth the words. To this day I think of her every time I read Romans 8.

"If God be for us, who can be against us? . . ."

"For I am persuaded, that neither death, nor life, nor angels, nor principalities, nor powers, nor things present, nor things to come,

Nor height, nor depth, nor any other creature, shall be able to separate us from the love of God, which is in Christ Jesus our Lord."

Romans 8: 31, 38, 39

Isma is standing below the side porch facing the lake, circa 1958.

Grandma Isma and Robert Frost

Kay Huffman Gregory

Daughter of Hal and Rachel Huffman

As a teenager, I soaked up Grandma's stories of her youth. One story stands out in my memory as it served me well in my teaching career.

One summer morning, I was sitting on Grandma's back porch helping her break green beans. She described the long ago Saturday activity when all the girls would wash their hair. Her description of the weekly process fascinated me because it was so unlike my own personal hair washing rituals. Like all the girls in my junior high school, I was accustomed to washing my hair every single day! Before I could think about taking a superior stance, Grandma quickly reminded me that when she was young, neither her family nor her entire rural community had indoor bathtubs and showers with flowing hot water.

According to Grandma, the Saturday hair washing was a social occasion where sisters and often their friends would gather to help each other achieve clean, freshly braided hair for attending church the next day. First long braids were patiently unwound, and the hair was brushed. Then the young ladies would dip their hair in a large pail of water drawn from the well. The dripping hair was then soaped and rinsed with freshly drawn well water.

Grandma said that once the hair was clean, the next task was to get it dried -- a challenge, as there was no electricity and no hair dryers to help. If it were a sunny day, the girls would spread out a blanket on the grass where the they would shift their long tresses to get various positions of the sun's warm drying rays. They would often kneel on their knees and spread their hair out in front of them on the blanket to dry. Once the back of their hair had dried, they would turn over and recline, spreading the front sections of their hair out around them like halos. When the clean hair was dried, there was the brushing out of tangles bringing the hair to a bright sheen and the elaborate braiding that would last until the next Saturday.

Years later when I was teaching American literature to college students, I totally understood the passage in Robert Frost's famous poem "Birches." Frost describes how the limber birch trees often get permanently bent down by the winter's weight of ice and snow saying:

> "You may see their trunks arching in the woods
> Years afterwards, trailing their leaves on the ground
> Like girls on hands and knees that throw their hair
> Before them over their heads to dry in the sun."

Thanks to Grandma Isma, I was always able to explain this part of the poem to my students, most arriving to class with freshly washed hair each morning.

Tamarack

Kay Huffman Gregory

Daughter of Hal and Rachel Huffman

When I was in the third grade, I had been longing for my very own pony for months and months. It was my ultimate dream, and I made sure my parents were very clear on that point. I had read every horse book I could locate in the Viewmont Elementary School Library, so I was sure that I would make a most excellent horse owner and a most skilled rider. All of those pages I had read practically guaranteed that. Right? All of my accumulated knowledge about horses would soon receive a reality check in the person of my Grandpa and my Daddy, and in the spirit of a lively, unbroken colt.

My dream came true. Daddy told me that I would soon have a young pony. My Grandpa Arthur Huffman had once worked as a real live cowboy out in Wyoming. I grew up on his adventuresome Wyoming stories, and I had great respect and absolute trust that he could train my new pony. Grandpa said we should call the pony Tamarack. He once had a horse named that. He said it was an Indian name from out West, the name of a pretty tree, so Tamarack it was.

Bursting with excitement, I could not wait to see my new pony that had been delivered to Grandpa Huffman's farm. My family had not yet moved out to Huffman's Cove, so we didn't have a place for Tamarack just yet. The first time I eagerly reached out to pet the pretty white blaze on his face, Tamarack gave me a pretty solid bite on the hand. Well, there was nothing in my books about biting horses! My enthusiasm was quickly tempered with actual fear of this very real (and to me) very huge animal, an animal that obviously was unaware that he was supposed to play the role of loving, loyal pet. Grandpa barked at me, "Kay, you will have to learn to show that pony who's boss! You will have to teach him how to behave." My anticipation was wavering towards fear and dread.

Weeks passed. While I watched, Grandpa worked frequently with Tamarack. First he broke him to lead with a halter. Then he introduced a bridle with a bit. Next, he placed a saddle on Tamarack's back and tightened the girth. Tamarack reared up on his hind legs briefly. Grandpa swiftly took care of that bad behavior with a sharp snap of the riding crop. "You have to show him who's boss," Grandpa growled. Tamarack complied, and secretly, I wanted to cry. I didn't like Grandpa hitting my pony. Yet, a pony rearing up on his hind legs was an even scarier proposition than Grandpa's discipline with the riding crop.

Grandpa worked with me too. He taught me how to lift up each of Tamarack's legs to clean out his hooves with the metal hoof pick. He showed me how to groom Tamarack with brushes and a mane pick. This I could do!

Before too long, Tamarack appeared very comfortable with carrying the saddle around on his back. He no longer got angry when the girth was tightened around his stomach, and Grandpa had started letting me sit on Tamarack while he led us around the yard. One Sunday afternoon, Grandpa and Daddy were leading Tamarack with me aboard down Grandpa's driveway. The drive was lined on both sides by pasture fence. At the bottom of the drive, Dad looked at me and said that it was time for me to ride Tamarack all by myself.

Daddy assured me that he and Grandpa would be following right behind, and Tamarack really couldn't go anywhere but back to the house. The minute Daddy unsnapped the lead, Tamarack shot up the driveway like he was leaving the race gates at the Kentucky Derby. My first solo ride was more a breathless, headlong gallop where I held on for dear life. When we reached the top of the hill and entered the flat driveway area, I was relieved that my wild ride was just about over.

For some reason, Tamarack had other ideas. He jumped down a low rock wall that marked the lower edge of the driveway and ran inside the chicken house with me still on his back. The chicken house had a low ceiling with a lot of spider webs, and the white chickens were squawking and flapping their wings. I just crouched low in the saddle and cried. All of my equestrian dreams appeared to end in the indignity of the chicken house!

Soon Grandpa and Daddy were in the chicken house too. If I was expecting sympathy from those two, I was wrong. "I want to get off," I wailed.

Daddy echoed my Grandpa. "No. You just stay right on that pony. You have got to show him who's boss!" Daddy led me out of the chicken house. He said, "Hold on. I will have him jump right up this wall." For all his good intentions, Daddy forgot that Grandma's clothesline ran along the wall where we were going to jump. Sure enough, Tamarack did jump back up the wall, and the clothesline caught in my mouth, dragging me off and to the ground.

Fortunately, none of these Sunday afternoon adventures caused me any serious physical harm. And yes, Daddy did make me get back on Tamarack that day to finish my ride over to the barn. I had a lot more to learn before Tamarack would accept me as "boss." I look back now and realize that Daddy and Grandpa were teaching me important life skills far beyond how to stay on a wild pony's back.

In just a few months, I was confident enough to ride Tamarack by myself without any chicken house detours. I brushed and groomed Tamarack until he absolutely sparkled in the sunlight. I borrowed some of Grandma's Suave Hair Crème to make his black mane and tail shimmer. Tamarack repaid all of my love and attention with his full acceptance of me. Secretly, I knew that I was not the "boss." Instead, we were partners. Our love for each other was mutual.

Soon I was entering Tamarack in local horse shows. It became a Saturday night family affair. I would spend most of the day giving Tamarack a bath and liberally applying more of Grandma's Suave hair crème to his mane and tail. Daddy would rush home from the hardware just in time to position the homemade rack in the back of the truck that served as our horse trailer. Then all six of us would pile into the cab of the truck with Tamarack tied in back and my saddle and gear tied to the sides of the truck rack. What I would give to have a picture of the whole family and Tamarack traveling down the road, barely making it to the show grounds in time to get registered and to saddle up for the competition.

I was still reading horse books with wild abandon, and anything I read about, I was sure that Tamarack and I could do. So when I read a book about a little girl who rode a jumping horse, I lugged cement blocks up to the riding ring and stacked them up, and then topped the construction with a broom handle for the jump. Tamarack, always the good sport, sailed right over this rather unsafe "jump." We soon tired of that exercise and moved on to other challenges.

By now, I knew the differences in gear and clothing for Western and English style riding. To that end, little by little I acquired the riding clothes for each. With a cowboy hat, jeans, and a pearl snap shirt, Tamarack and I entered many Western Pleasure pony classes. We won first place several times. After putting the ponies through their paces, the competitors "parked" their ponies in the center of the ring awaiting a close inspection by the judge. At the judge's command, each competitor would be told to back her pony. Many ponies would toss their heads and refuse to hit reverse. Or they would side step instead of a smooth reverse and then forward. Not Tamarack. We would glide back and forth as if operated by remote control. In our Western garb, we also entered the occasional pony race, and once we even placed third in a barrel race.

Some evenings, we would compete in both the Western Pleasure Pony class and the English Pleasure Pony class by simply changing Tamarack's

Kay is with horse "Mike" and Chip is riding the beloved "Tamarack," 1962. Note my mixed Western wear with English jodhpurs!

saddle and my clothing. There were no rules about these things back then, but I'll bet the judge at least had to appreciate our flexibility. In my mind, Tamarack could do anything.

Somewhere, I read that to excel, a horse and rider needed to work out regularly. The summer when I was twelve, I decided that Tamarack and I should ride early in the morning before it got hot. I rose at 5:00, quietly slipped out of the sleeping house, and went to the barn to saddle up.

Those early morning rides were magical. There was often mist rising off the lake, and we left tracks in the dewy grass along the side of the road. There were not many homes along Huffman's Cove Road back then, and there were a lot more forested areas. I remember the dappled sunlight scattering along the ground as we passed by, the only sounds the morning birds, an excited dog barking in the distance, and Tamarack's hoof beats. It was a time of quiet beauty and a time of dreams and endless possibilities.

Tamarack lived to be thirty-two years old. Over the years, Dad purchased other horses, but Tamarack was the special one. Dad always said that Tamarack would have a place to live on Huffman's Cove for the remainder of his life, and he did. Both of my children got to ride on the back of a very old Tamarack in 1988. Tamarack enriched my life, and helped me to forge a special bond with both my father and my cowboy grandfather.

Hal's grandchildren enjoy Tamarack in 1988.

Acknowledgements

I am grateful to the many individuals who contributed to the completion of this book. A big thank you goes to all my first cousins and my siblings who graciously spent the time to write down fond memories of our incredible grandparents, Isma and Arthur Huffman.

Next I am indebted to my sisters Beth Huffman and Mandy Hall for patiently listening to my endless talk about plans for this book. You're the best! Mandy also served as a dedicated proofreader, editorial advisor, and photography consultant for this project.

Then there is my "other sister" – my longtime friend Becky Hart also provided careful proofreading and astute editorial suggestions. Thanks, Becky! I am also very grateful for poet Tim Peeler's insightful editing.

Millie Kate Huffman Griswold, Arthur and Isma's youngest child, has served as family historian for many years. Millie very generously shared her extensive family photograph collection as well as her first-hand knowledge of life on Huffman's Cove. She was always prompt to help locate detailed answers to questions I posed.

Another thank you goes to Jeanette Huffman, Forest's wife, who was also a great source of information for this book.

And finally, I am grateful for my ancestors who obviously loved to take photographs. The historic family photographic record further accentuates the experiences woven into this book. Most of all, I hold a huge debt of gratitude to Isma Moretz Huffman for her gift of family memories. Thanks, Grandma!

About the Editor

Kay Huffman Gregory had the pleasure of growing up on Huffman's Cove just a short walk from the home of her paternal grandparents, Isma and Arthur Huffman, whose lives are detailed in this book.

Kay holds both an undergraduate and a Master's degree in English. Most of her forty years in education were spent at the university and community college level. For the final five years of her career, she served as Dean of the School of Academics, Education, and Fine Arts at Catawba Valley Community College.

Kay enjoys spending time with her children and grandchildren. She also enjoys reading, gardening, and photography. Here she visits with her grandchildren.

Made in the USA
Columbia, SC
15 October 2022